Speaking of Stress Management through Yoga and Meditation

The book deals with the problems of stress of modern living and provides guidelines for securing release from the bondage of thoughts, feelings and reflexes. The yogic process is essentially psychosomatic. An integrated health-care programme is prescribed in the book. It has been scientifically evaluated and tested for more than two decades and is based on four distinct elements of yoga technology. There are simple meditative postures to bring about inwardness of the mind. Therapeutic asanas are carefully selected for release of tension from the muscular and nervous systems and discomfort from the body. Techniques of simplified *pranayamas* are included to promote inner peace and cheerfulness.

The book shall prove to be of special value to psychologists, psychotherapists and yoga teachers, overstressed busy executives and overworked physicians who want to seek release from tension and enjoy freedom, happiness and peace in this age of competition, restlessness, anxiety and fear.

Pandit Shambhu Nath was a senior teacher of Yoga Education at the Yoga Institute of Santa Cruz, Bombay. He was a lecturer at the Film and TV Institute, Pune (1963-1970). He organised "Better Living" courses in Bombay, Madras, Goa, Rajasthan and Delhi (1970-74). He was Course Director, Academy of Yoga and Research, Bharatiya Vidya Bhawan, Delhi branch (1975-1991).

Pandit Shambhu Nath was Junior Research Fellow in the Orthopaedic Department of the All India Institute of Medical Sciences (AIIMS) and conducted group therapy in two phases: 1977-78 and 1979-81. Appointed Yoga Instructor in the Department of Psychiatry, AIIMS, he conducted a two-year research project, "Yoga Therapy with Anxiety Neurotics" (1986-88), and a three-year project, "Comparative Study of Progressive Relaxation and Yogic Relaxation Techniques in the Management of Anxiety Neurotics" (1989-1991), both sponsored by the Indian Council of Medical Research. He was a Founder Trustee of Shri Yogendra Yoga Foundation, New Delhi and Jodhpur, and a Founder-member of the International Board of Yoga, Yoga Bhawan, Mumbai.

But unfortunately, he is no longer amidst us.

speaking of
Stress Management through Yoga and Meditation

Pandit Shambhu Nath

NEW DAWN PRESS, INC.
USA• UK• INDIA

STERLING PAPERBACKS
An imprint of
Sterling Publishers (P) Ltd.
A-59, Okhla Industrial Area, Phase-II,
New Delhi-110020.
Tel: 26387070, 26386209; Fax: 91-11-26383788
E-mail: mail@sterlingpublishers.com
www.sterlingpublishers.com

Speaking of Stress Management through Yoga and Meditation
© 2005, Sterling Publishers (P) Ltd.
ISBN 978 81 207 7805 4
Reprint 2006, 2009, 2012

All rights are reserved.
No part of this publication may be reproduced, stored in a retrieval system or transmitted, in any form or by any means, mechanical, photocopying, recording or otherwise, without prior written permission of the original publisher.

Printed in India

Printed and Published by Sterling Publishers Pvt. Ltd.,
New Delhi-110 020.

*Dedicated to
The Yoga Institute, Bombay,
my Alma Mater
with a deep sense of
gratitude and love*

Yoga which studied man in depth at all levels has much to offer to project an alternative to the modern style of thinking and living. What is needed is to understand Yoga not as others understand it but as Patanjali understood and propagated it. In his classic system of Yoga, he has methodically shown what afflictions man suffers from and for what reasons. He has applied spiritual psychology to explore this and has supplied the basic technology for elevating man from his moorings of animal life. Those working for sublimation, integration and evolution of man will have no better alternative than the acceptance of Yoga as a way of life for future generations.

— Shri Yogendraji

FOREWORD

Pandit Shambhu Nath was a fine product of the Yoga Institute, Santa Cruz, Bombay, an institute that has devoted itself for the last 70 years to the popularisation of Yoga in a systematic and scientific way. People like Pandit Shambhu Nath who have been associated with the Yoga Institute as part of its faculty for many years can be easily distinguished. Such people are sincere and dedicated, and it takes just a little while to realise the difference between peddlers of spirituality and pseudo-yogins and genuine teachers of yoga. When such a committed teacher of yoga decides to write a book about his experience of many years, the product becomes significant and intrinsically valuable. It matters little if Pandit Shambhu Nath was not a literary wizard so long as what he wrote was useful and understood by a busy executive, an overworked physician or an overstressed artist or worker. I am sure this book will be found helpful by intellectuals who are not acquainted with Yoga but who would like to read and practise something simple that can mean good health, mental tranquillity and spiritual poise.

Dr Jayadeva Yogendra

ACKNOWLEDGMENTS

I express my deep debt of gratitude to Dr Jayadevaji Yogendra, Principal of the Yoga Institute, Santa Cruz, Bombay, who not only taught me all that I know of Yoga but has been to me a friend, philosopher and guide; and to Smt Hansa Yogendra for her valuable suggestions and encouragement.

I am also grateful to Mother Sita Devi but for whose guidance, love and affection, I would not have ventured to write this book.

My special thanks are due to Justice H. L. Anand for writing the introduction.

My gratitude are due to Dr P. K. D. Shah, Dr Shekhar Saxena, Dr H. M. Chawla and Dr Gurminder Sahasi for their valuable contributions to the first part of the book.

PREFACE

The present trend of thought based on a materialistic philosophy of power, prosperity and pleasure has resulted in a form of sensate culture. Worldly values dominate the modern man, who reacts to stimuli, struggles for self-preservation, self-aggrandisement and self-gratification. This ego-ridden individual seeks freedom and happiness in his nerve-racking hunt after worldly objects in the external world which leads to a life of bondage, misery, worries, insecurity, despair, frustration, disillusionment and doubt. The modern man has sold himself out to gain reputation, personal power, more money, selfish ends; he is caught in a never-ending mad rat-race to meet all kinds of unrestrained needs which wear out, tear out, destroy his vital organs much sooner than before due to his abnormal living habits, strenuous and overstressed life. We overstrain this human machine, and then either the body or the mind breaks down. We disregard nature's warnings. All this leads to disintegration of personalities which is expressed in so many psychiatric and psychosomatic disturbances. At least 72 per cent of diseases in metropolitan cities are psychosomatic diseases or stress related diseases, associated with mental or emotional disturbances.

The modern man needs to be re-educated to find the basis of a healthy and satisfying life, a creative and meaningful life, a life which is tension-free and gives him real freedom, happiness and peace. Yoga, the science of man, based on ancient Indian wisdom and culture, is an art *par excellence* of living a healthy, balanced, peaceful and contented life. Yoga, being a total integrated system, studies man in his wholeness—body, mind and spirit and is wedded to certain intrinsic principles, ideas, values, attitudes and a way of life for personal and social benefit.

"Yoga suggests an integrated approach to man with the personality-complex (*chitta*) as the basic factor and treats man as a body-mind complex." If the *chitta* is to play its larger role today, it is in the field of reintegration and restructuring of man's personality to bring about a qualitative change in him from the ignoble to the noble. The practical system of yoga aims at the psychosomatic discipline, meditation and spiritual consciousness.

This book presents an Integrated Health Care course based on Classical Yoga techniques with its variegated elements of yoga technology for harmonising and reintegrating the individual's personality at all levels of consciousness—physical, mental, moral, intellectual, emotional and spiritual.

This Health Care Course has been tested for more than a decade at the Academy of Yoga and Research, Bharatiya Vidya Bhavan (Delhi Branch). It was also applied to patients suffering from anxiety, as an exploratory study in the Department of Psychiatry, All India Institute of Medical Sciences (AIIMS), sponsored by the Indian Council of Medical Research, New Delhi. The results have been very encouraging and thousands of students belonging to all age groups and walks of life have benefited from it.

Simple therapeutic *asanas* have been carefully selected, based on the principle of relaxation. These are to be performed following a well-defined pattern of rhythmic breathing for reducing stress. They create a positive feeling, steadiness and comfort.

Standardised techniques of simple *pranayamas* (breathing process) are included to improve one's breathing, making it harmonious and deep, which has a sedative effect on the nerves and brings about mental equilibrium. Special psychosomatic practices are there to give one a feeling of let go and complete neuro-muscular relaxation. Practices to condition the mind and meditation techniques are prescribed for gaining quietude, stillness of the mind and silence. These help in developing a state of peace and tranquillity. Devotion and surrender to God is of help in meditation — "Be still and know God", says the scriptures. The importance of diet reform from yogic as well as a commonsensical point of view is stressed.

A separate section deals with mental and emotional therapeutics and with the four basic destructive emotions: anger, jealousy, fear and worry, and depression. One can heal the mind by contemplation and thought power. A positive, hopeful, constructive mental attitude has to be cultivated. The right attitude of mind and a belief in a higher benevolent reality are vital in Yoga which gives one courage, confidence, fortitude, steadfastness and strength. All this helps to develop an objective attitude to life and leads to a gradual change in one's habitual reaction pattern, a better control of one's personality and enables one to lead a tension-free life. The book contains useful suggestions and guidance for self-improvement, reflection and understanding of life.

The book will be of special interest to Yoga teachers, counsellors and those suffering from stressful conditions of anxiety and tension and will prove equally useful to the layman and the uninitiated.

It is the purpose of yoga to free the personality-complex from the bondage of thoughts, feelings and reflexes which have accumulated in the subconscious. Only then is it possible for us to have a balanced mind or intellect.

— Shri Yogendraji

For Right Living
— We must eat the right kind of food (*ahar*).
— We must carefully work out a regime of yogic exercises (*vihar*).
— We must have the right habits, attitude and code of conduct (*achar*).
— We must have the right kind of thoughts (*vichar*)
  Our well-being is based on these four factors of *ahar, vihar, achar* and *vichar*.

Pandit Shambhu Nath

CONTENTS

Foreword	*vii*
Acknowledgements	*viii*
Preface	*ix*
Introduction	*xv*

PART I
Physical and Emotional Responses to Stress

1.	Physical Response to Stress Dr P. K. D. Shah	3
2.	Anxiety and its Effects on Health Dr Shekhar Saxena	6
3.	Emotions and Stress Dr Gurminder K. Sahasi & Dr H. M. Chawla	10

PART II
Yoga and the System and its Methodology

4.	Classical Yoga	23
5.	Psychosomatic Approach to Yoga	26

PART III
Integrated Health Care Programme

6.	Ill health means Disharmony	33
7.	Handling the Body-Mind Complex	35
8.	The Preparation and Conditioning of the Mind	36
9.	Restoring Balance and Rhythm for Inner Harmony	41
10.	The Basic Ideal	42
11.	Guidelines for Performance	44
12.	Therapeutic Postures	45
13.	Simplified Pranayamas (Breathing Process)	55
14.	Yogic Complete Breath	57
15.	Pranayama Practices can Help in Many Ways	58

16. General Precautions	59
17. Create Rhythm of Breath to Harmonise Thoughts	60
18. Means of Relaxation	68
19. Psychosomatic Practices	71
20. Food and Yoga	75

PART IV
Your Stress Factor

21. Psychosomatic Problems	85
22. Emotional States Affect the Body's Defences	87
23. Internally Generated Pressure	90

PART V
A Technique for
Achieving Inner Tranquillity (Meditation)

24. Tranquillity Provides a Backdrop	95
25. Meditation	99
26. Meditate to Open Yourself to the Divine Power	103

PART VI
Thought Control and Emotional Therapeutics

27. Thoughts are Forces	109
28. Emotional Control	111
29. Our Destructive Emotions	113

PART VII
Guidelines for Living a Fuller Life

30. How to Carry on Your Work (Your Action Potential)	119
31. The Importance of Karma Yoga	122
32. Attitude of Mind is Vital in Yoga	124
33. On Faith	127
34. Belief in a Higher Benevolent Reality	128
35. Steps for Self-Improvement	130
Epilogue	134
Appendix	143
Bibliography	

INTRODUCTION

We live in an age of crises. There is a crisis of character and discipline. There is a crisis of faith. There is large-scale erosion of values. There is widespread corruption in all walks of life. At all levels, enforced discipline has totally failed threatening the very fabric of life. The dimensions of the crises make them almost appear civilisational in nature posing a threat not only to all value systems but to life itself.

It is but proper that in such a situation, sensitive and thoughtful people should ponder over the problem and devise ways and means to arrest the rot, rehabilitate the degenerating man, start a process of reconstruction of society, raise the moral tone of the people and the quality of life and enrich life on earth even while the Homo sapiens may be left free to carry on their pursuit for material prosperity and happiness.

Yoga, one of the six systems of Indian philosophy and a part of the ancient Indian mysticism which was passed on from the master to the disciple as a sacred and secret wisdom in the hermitage, represents both the highest goal that man could achieve as well as the instrument through which it could be done. Conceived by the great sages in their quest for self-realisation, it has come to be recognised, during its long travails from the hermitages to the cities, as the science of man, a philosophy of life, a code of conduct, an attitude and an approach, as well as an art of living which is capable not only of ensuring physical well-being, mental peace, harmony, moral elevation and spiritual upliftment of man but also of transforming man from his gross animal existence to the sublime heights of divinity. In the words of Sri Aurobindo, Yoga puts the instruments of evolution itself into the hands of man and thereby makes him an architect of his own destiny. It is a system of self-discipline which is capable of introducing an element of harmony in the life of man, who is torn by conflicts, tensions, greed, avarice, jealousy, hatred, exaggerated ego and the pursuit of material objects. Yoga has a very wide and comprehensive sweep and is multidimensional. Whether it is Raja Yoga, Hatha Yoga, Gyana Yoga, Dhyana Yoga, Bhakti Yoga, Kundalini Yoga or any other form of yoga, the emphasis is on the control of mind, the steadying of the mind, subordinating it to the superintellect, the highest consciousness and the claim of the soul. All human actions, whatever be their motivation, are the result of the play of the mind and an unregulated, uncontrolled mind causes pain and even disaster. Yoga, therefore, introduces an insulating element between the mind and action and ensures reasoned action, balance in action, virtuous action and value-oriented action. It is, thus, possible to tame the mind in course of time and keep man on the path of rectitude, purity and good.

It is, however, necessary to bear in mind the dynamic role of yoga as an instrument of evolution and therefore, of growth and development, both material and spiritual. It is also good to remember that the need for equanimity must also be understood not as resignation or acceptance of fate but in its positivistic quality of ensuring fairness and justness in all your dealings and in your numerous relationships and embodying a quality of evenness of temper and a mental balance in the face of the stresses and strains of life. It, however, does not mean insensitivity to the challenges of the modern age. These challenges must, however, continue to agitate our minds so that they are squarely met in an effort to raise the quality of life. The challenges should not disturb the mind but reinforce it, egging it on to better effort and excellence in the field of action as symbolised by the *Gita* — "Yogas karmasukaushalam".

When we talk of yoga, it must, however, be kept in mind that it is a long and arduous journey calling for perseverance, persistence, dedication and total surrender. There is no instant yoga. It is not a question of merely closing one's eyes or of sitting in a posture. It involves cultivation of attitude and approach to life. It must not only be a philosophy to be imbibed but a practical philosophy which must be lived. It is, therefore, not enough to think of yoga but to do it and to live it in our lives. It is also necessary to understand that yoga is not a substitute formation. Human effort is indispensable. The transformation we talk of is not at the cost of action but it enables us to perform our duties more efficiently, more effectively and honestly.

Man may or may not have a 'mind of his own', he may or may not be able 'to mind' his business in difficult areas of life amidst the pursuit of worldly pleasures, and the play of his sensory perceptions; and may be guilty of 'mindless' thoughts, utterances, and actions, and thus may cause pain and misery to himself, his fellow human beings, the other members of the living species, and may even embark on a suicidal course of destruction of life on earth; yet man is man because he has a 'mind', a faculty that nature exclusively bestowed on him in the course of evolution from the animal-like state and thus placed this chosen species at the pinnacle of the earthly system. The divine gift of mind has not, however, been an unmixed blessing. While man has achieved material prosperity, developed scientific and technological skills, and through their intelligent use, accelerated the pace of growth in an attempt to improve the standard of living, if not the quality of life, the mind has at the same time been responsible for widespread misery and pain in life. The mind was thus recognised as the greatest tormentor of man which has the potential to infect the body and even to destroy it. The ancient seers had realised this potential when the system of self-discipline of the mind was evolved to enable man to contain its potential to cause mischief. The modern researchers in the constant pursuit and evaluation of ancient wisdoms recognised this when they confirmed, on the basis of laboratory tests and experiments with various forms of life, the concept of 'mind-made diseases', ie., physical problems of the body created by the mind. Recent researches have led to a more positive approach to the mind-body interaction and it is being increasingly realised, and has been established by research, that the mind that torments is also capable, in its finer and higher states, to rid man of his agony, and even bring him close to ecstasy. This is the new concept of 'mind-made health'. That the mind, which torments, can also liberate, is no more an enigma or a mystery because the mind has many dimensions, layers and levels; from the gross or the animal level to the human, the superhuman and even the divine, and the cosmic level. What you may do to yourself and the world around you and what the human mind may do or undo for you and the world would depend on the level of the mind or consciousness at which you operate and are established. The highest level of the mind and the most refined of its states is capable of achievement within a lifetime by the process of self-discipline. Once you operate at the finer levels of consciousness you can raise yourself to great heights. Maintenance of a sound body and health is one of its many minor advantages. You can, therefore, raise the level of your mind by conscious effort and *Saadhna* and thereby not only ensure good health but also progress on the path to eternal bliss, health which has not merely physical but also a spiritual dimension.

At one time, not in the distant past, science and spirituality were considered poles apart. Recent developments, however, indicate a growing realisation that even though their methods of enquiry and the tools are different, both science and spirituality are engaged in the common quest to unravel the mysteries of the 'unknown' and even the 'unknowable', with a view to a better understanding of the problems and prospects of mankind, so as to accelerate the pace of evolution, ensure physical fitness, mental peace, and thereby improve the quality of life. The papers, contributed by the scientists and scholars from different disciplines have been made possible by the pioneering and untiring efforts of Pandit Shambhu Nath, who was a proud product of the Yoga Institute, Bombay. They are a clear pointer to the need for, and the benefits of, further interaction between science and spirituality in their common endeavour to usher in a new era of peace and understanding.

H. L. Anand

Part I
Physical and Emotional Responses to Stress

1
Physical Response to Stress

Dr P. K. D. Shah

The word 'stress' in common English usage means conditions causing hardship or times of trouble, danger and tension. This term in medicine has many different connotations. It may be best used to denote psychosocial situations including physical and mental illnesses which can produce disorganisation of behaviour. Stress can be defined "as stimulus or change in the external or internal environment in terms of strength, intensity or duration, so as to tax the adaptive capacity of the organism to its limit, and which, in certain circumstances, can lead to a disorganisation of behaviour or maladaptation or a dysfunction which may lead to diseases." (Rees, 1988).

It is evident, therefore, that both bodily illnesses, physical situations like exposure to extremes of temperature, etc., and psychosocial aberrations could constitute stress for an individual. In case of physical stress the severity of illness or situation would decide the bodily response to that stress. On the other hand, the power or force of psychosocial stress is determined by the individual's perception regarding its capacity to challenge or threaten his well-being. The response to such a situation would largely be affective and may vary from denial, displacement to rationalisation and self-deception.

Whatever be it, the body does respond in a definite manner to any stressful situation.

The physical response to stress involves three systems:
- The Autonomic Nervous System
- The Endocrine System
- The Muscular System or the Skeletal System

The Autonomic Nervous System

This comprises sympathetic and parasympathetic divisions which have opposite actions on various organs but work in tandem to the benefit of the individual. As a response to stress there is stimulation of the sympathetic system. This increases alertness of the individual and prepares him to cope with the stress in a better manner. Under the influence of increased sympathetic activity large amounts of adrenaline and noradrenaline which are secreted by the medullary portion of the adrenal gland are released into the circulation of the blood.

The overall physiological effect of this is that there is a redistribution of blood, with more blood going to the skeletal muscles and the brain preparing them for strenuous physical activity. The blood pressure of the person rises and the pulse beats at a faster rate. There is an overall increase in mental activity. The rate of cellular metabolism increases and the blood glucose values rise.

Stimulation of the sympathetic system in response to an emotional state is mediated through a portion of the brain called the hypothalamus which controls such subtle functions as emotions, food intake and sex drive.

The Endocrine System

The endocrine system of the body, which is concerned with the secretions of hormones, also gets modulated under stress. Hormones serve important vital functions in the body; it raises the level of growth hormones secreted by the pituitary gland situated at the base of the skull. There is increased activity of the adrenals, and large amounts of its active hormone, cortisol, is secreted. During a severe physical stressful situation like trauma, surgery, acute severe infection, as much as of 300 mg of hormone may be secreted as against an average daily limit of 37 mg. Levels of thyroxine also rise in the blood. This hormone is secreted by the thyroid gland and regulates the rate of metabolic activities of the body. Under the influence of these, and adrenaline, noradrenaline and the body glucose which is stored as glycogen, gets converted into glucose—the readily available fuel—in order to meet the extra requirements of the individual.

The Skeletal System

During the period of stress there is increased tension in the skeletal muscles. This continued increased tension is often manifested in the form of generalised body pains of which patients of anxiety and psychiatric disorders complain.

H. Selye described a syndrome of adaptation to various types of stress and this is commonly known as General Adaptation Syndrome. This has three stages:
- Alarm Reaction
- Stage of Resistance
- Stage of Exhaustion

The alarm reaction is characterised by neural mechanism, sympathetic overactivity, release of adrenal medullary and cortical hormones.

The stage of resistance is characterised by an increase in the size of adrenal gland, increased secretion of cortisol, increased activity of the thyroid and protein anabolism.

If the stress is prolonged, the adaptation fails to keep pace and this happens in the stage of exhaustion.

In this manner various body responses allow the individual to cope with stress which may be physical or psychosocial.

2
Anxiety and its Effects on Health

Dr Shekhar Sexena

What is Anxiety?

We experience a variety of emotions at various stages in our lives. Anxiety is one of the most frequent of such emotions. All of us have experienced it. Psychologists define it "as the fearful anticipation of an unpleasant event in the future". According to this definition anxiety is similar to fear, but this fear is about something unknown in the future. Anxiety is almost always unpleasant and uncomfortable.

Anxiety is caused by something intangible, while fear is usually due to something which is real and threatening. Similarly, anxiety largely arises because of our internal psychological interpretation of a threatening situation, while fear is usually caused by an external realistic danger. For this reason, different persons may have very different levels of anxiety when facing the same situation.

Anxiety is also the result of psychological stress. An imminent examination or interview, an anticipated rebuke by a senior at work, worries about financial problems, all of them produce anxiety.

Viewed this way, anxiety is a common but non-specific response to stress. It is a signal indicating that there is some threat to the person. In this respect anxiety in the mind is just like fever in the body. Fever can be caused by a number of illnesses and indicates non-specifically that something is going wrong in the body. Similarly, anxiety can be a response to any kind of psychological threat or stress.

We all have different levels of baseline anxiety. Some of us have a low level of anxiety, while others have a high level. This baseline level of anxiety is governed by our personality. In addition, different situations induce varying extents of increase in anxiety. While some amount of increase in anxiety is adaptive, and helps us to recognise and respond to dangers, a persistently high level becomes maladaptive and interferes with our functioning. When anxiety remains high on a sustained basis and produces significant distress to a person and disability in his functioning, it is termed *Anxiety Disorder*. A persistently high level of anxiety can significantly endanger his mental and physical well-being.

The Psychological Manifestations of Anxiety

Anxiety is primarily a psychological experience. Besides the unpleasant fear which is central to anxiety, a number of other psychological symptoms accompany it. There is decreased concentration, excessive worries, tensions and brooding, and an inability to take decisions. Interest in work and leisure activities may decrease. The person may become restless and he may not feel relaxed even while resting. Irritability is increased and even ordinary noise may upset an anxious person. If anxiety becomes severe, the person may temporarily lose control over himself. This state is called *Pranic Reaction*. Prolonged anxiety can induce mental depression also.

The Physical Manifestations of Anxiety

Anxiety also induces a number of changes in the body. Quite often, people with high anxiety seek help from doctors primarily for these bodily symptoms. These include:

Palpitation, chest discomfort and pain, increased blood pressure, and an empty feeling in the chest and stomach. Breathing may become rapid, and the anxious person may complain of choking and inability to hold his breath. Hyperacidity symptoms are quite common.

An anxious person has a desire to pass urine frequently and may have loose motions. Muscles become tense and stiff and this can result in aches and pain in various parts of the body. Hands and feet may tremble and become cold. If anxiety becomes severe, the person may experience dizziness, unsteadiness and might even faint.

One of the most frequent early symptoms of anxiety is disturbed sleep. An anxious person takes a longer time to sleep and may wake up several times during the night. Sleep may also be full of dreams and nightmares, hence not refreshing.

The Vicious Cycle of Anxiety

Once anxiety sets in, it can perpetuate itself by a vicious cycle. Anxiety gives rise to physical symptoms as described earlier. As these symptoms appear to indicate serious physical illnesses like heart or chest diseases to the person, he becomes more anxious. This way anxiety can reach a high level within a short time and can perpetuate itself even after the initial causal factor has disappeared.

Effects of Anxiety on Health

Sustained anxiety induces changes in the body, and can lead to a large number of diseases. These are sometimes grouped under the broad heading of psychosomatic diseases, as psychological factors, mainly anxiety, are responsible for somatic diseases. Foremost among these diseases are cardiac and vascular diseases like high blood pressure, coronary artery diseases and cardiac arrhythmias. Rise in blood pressure is a direct effect of anxiety and if it becomes chronic, hypertension can result. Similarly, anxiety is also an important risk factor for coronary artery diseases which manifests as angina pectoris, myocardial infarction and sudden death. These are some of the leading causes of death all over the world. Anxiety can result in irregular heartbeats also, which is itself a serious disease.

The role of anxiety in bronchial asthma and peptic ulcers is also well established. Asthma attacks are quite often precipitated by anxiety-provoking situations. Many diseases of the gastrointestinal organs, including irritable bowel syndrome, are caused at least partly by psychological anxiety. A special kind of skin disease called neurodermatitis is related to anxiety and nervous scratching.

In women, menstrual disturbances, sterility, frequent abortions and premature childbirth may be related to anxiety. Anxiety can also lead to disturbances in eating. In some individuals anxiety gives rise to decreased appetite and weight, while in some others it tends to make them eat more. The latter can result in the problem of obesity which can increase the risk of many other serious illnesses.

Thinking that anxiety gets at least temporarily relieved with the use of alcohol and some drugs, a chronically anxious person may start using them. Over a period of time this can grow into a habit and then an addiction. One ought to abstain from alcohol and drugs under all circumstances.

Treatment of Anxiety Disorders

If anxiety becomes severe and sustained and affects one's health, it needs to be treated. Medicines are now available which have a specific anti-anxiety action. These medicines can reduce anxiety to a level which is more compatible with optimal functioning of the person and have wide applicability. However, their action is usually temporary. They may become ineffective over a longer period of time. Moreover, the person may become habituated to these medicines, making the cure worse than the disease. For these reasons medicines are not recommended for long-term use.

Several varieties of psychological therapies are available for reduction of anxiety. Some of them go deeper into the causes of anxiety while others attempt to ameliorate the manifestation of anxiety. These psychological treatments require a trained therapist and considerable time. Certain self-learning techniques for relaxation are also available which are easy and quite effective.

Recently, much research has been conducted on the usefulness of certain bio-feedback techniques in the control of excessive anxiety. There is also a revival of interest in the efficacy of meditation and yoga for anxiety disorders.

3
Emotions and Stress

Dr Gurminder K. Sahasi and Dr H. M. Chawla

> *Men are not disturbed by things,*
> *but by the views they take of them*
>
> (Epictetus, AD 60)

Although some philosophers have considered emotions as villains that represent what is most irrational and "animal-like" in human nature, there is a strong argument for crediting the emotions with all that is worthy and wonderful about human life. If 'love makes the world go around', it can also be said that, like love, many other emotions inspire us to improve our own lives and those of others.

Emotions cover a wide spectrum; they add colour and spice to our world of experience. Having emotions makes human life less tidy and predictable, but without them, the world would be drab and spiritless. Our conscious lives are governed by feelings of love, joy, anger, fear, jealousy and many other experiences. Psychodynamic theorists suggest that emotions are an important part of the unconscious underworld that affects our behaviour.

Emotions always have objects; they do not occur in a vacuum. We cannot simply be in love, feel happy, angry, fearful or proud. We are in love with someone, feel happy over something, angry at someone, fearful or proud of someone or something.

If the object of the emotion is adjudged as desirable or beneficial, we might feel happy or delighted if the object is present. We desire and wish for it if the object is not around. Appraising an object as undesirable, threatening or harmful, triggers negative emotions of fear, dislike or hatred (Lazarus, 1984). We may not always be consciously aware of the internal evaluations that underlie our emotional responses. There are more than 550 words in the English language that refer to various emotional states (Averill, 1980). Despite their diversity, emotions share common features which may differ from person to person and from culture to culture. When a person responds to an emotional stimulus, there are, first of all, thoughts about the situation and the meaning attached to it (eliciting stimuli—the events that arouse the emotion). Secondly, the person's interpretation of the situation, which gives meaning to it (cognitive appraisal). Thirdly, there is a state of physiological or bodily arousal. Finally, there are certain behavioural tendencies which may be expressive (for example, smiling or crying) or instrumental (ways of reacting to the stimulus that arouses the emotion), for example, by attacking or running away.

Cultural learning and individual life experiences help mould our appraisals. Growing in a specific culture determines how easily particular objects or people arouse emotions.

Clinical psychologist, Elbert Ellis, suggests that some commonly held beliefs are irrational and self-defeating because they lead to unnecessary emotional distress (Ellis & Grieger, 1977). The most basic belief among these perhaps is that it is terrible and catastrophic when things and people (including ourselves) do not turn out the way we expect them to be. Irrationality of this idea is seen by Ellis in two ways; (1) Things are seldom awful or catastrophic (they are merely annoying and frustrating); (2) It is self-defeating to turn our preferences and wants into absolute necessities. People who think in this manner tend to overreact with strong negative emotions of anger, depression and fear, when things or people are not necessarily the way they are expected to be.

Recent research has shown that the strongest predictors of personal happiness are cognitive rather than environmental. How people compare their own lifestyles and possessions with those of their past and future aspirations or, of others around them determine their state of mind. Existing objective factors like status, income, and marital status are less important in determining how happy they are (Diener, 1984).

The basic idea behind cognitive appraisal is dependent on the thoughts that shape our feelings (as you think, so shall you feel). Emotions are responses to our perceptions of the events and people around us. And the act of perception involves attaching meaning to sensations, thoughts, judgements and interpretations, creating a psychological reality to which we respond.

The idea that emotional reactions are triggered by cognitive appraisal rather than by external events accounts for the fact that different people (or even the same person at different times) may have different emotional reactions to the same object or person. Subjective interpretation of reality is internal in all perceptions but the appraisals involved in emotional behaviour are essentially 'evaluative and personal'; they relate to what we consider desirable or undesirable either for ourselves or for the people we care for (Averill, 1980).

External as well as internal stimuli may trigger our emotional responses. It is easier to identify the external events and situations that influence our emotional state and resulting behaviour but it is more difficult at times to identify the source of internal distress. At some time or the other, all of us may have felt anxious or 'down in the dumps' without knowing why.

The Physical Component

When our emotions are stirred up, the resultant physiological arousal is obviously noticeable. Many parts of the body are involved in emotional arousal. Psychophysiologists consider the nervous system and the endocrine system as especially significant in producing the physiological arousal that is identified with emotions.

Increased activity of the sympathetic nervous system helps the body deal with threatening situations like an emergency reaction or the flight or fight response. In contrast to the emergency reaction during anger or fear there are bodily reactions while relaxing or remaining calm. The pattern of bodily response during relaxation includes decreased activity of the sympathetic and somatic nervous system with increased parasympathetic activity. This is the maintenance system of the body which is responsible for conservation and replenishment of energy.

The Autonomic System

This consists of many nerves leading from the brain and spinal cord to the smooth muscles of the various organs of the body—heart, certain glands and to the blood vessels serving both the interior and exterior of the body. The autonomic nervous system has two parts. One part, the sympathetic system, is active during arousal states and prepares the body for extensive action by increasing the heart rate, raising the blood pressure, increasing the blood sugar level and raising the levels of certain hormones in the blood. It is this part of the autonomic nervous system that is active while we experience strong emotions such as fear and anger. It releases the hormone epinephrine (adrenaline) and norepinephrine (noradrenaline). Nerve impulses in the sympathetic system which reach the inner part of the adrenal glands, located above the kidneys, trigger the secretions of these hormones, which then enter the bloodstream and circulate. Epinephrine helps the functioning of liver to mobilise glucose into the blood, making energy available to the brain the muscles. It makes the heart beat faster (surgeons use epinephrine to stimulate heart action, when the heart is weakened or stopped). Epinephrine also duplicates and strengthens many of the actions of the sympathetic system. The other part of the autonomic nervous system tends to be active when we are calm and relaxed. It helps to build up and store the body's energy. For example, it decreases the heart rate, reduces the blood pressure and diverts blood to the digestive system. In aroused emotional states, sympathetic activity dominates; while in calmer states, parasympathetic activity is more prominent. But both systems can be active in many emotional states; for example in anger, the heart rate increases (a sympathetic effect) and so does digestive activity (a parasympathetic effect).

The Brain and the Emotions

Perception and evaluation of the situations that give rise to emotions and its physiological expression are controlled by the brain. A number of structures in the core of the brain are directly involved in regulating and coordinating the activity patterns characteristic of fear, anger and pleasure. These core parts of the brain include hypothalamus and a complex group of structures known as the limbic system. The structures of this system forms a ring, or border, around the brain stem as it enters the forebrain. Electrical stimulation of certain areas of the limbic system produces unrestrained aggression in animals. Destruction of the same sites cause absence of aggression, even if the animal is provoked or attacked (Kolb and Whishaw, 1985).

The aroused state caused by strong emotions is due to the increased activation of brain cells in the cerebral cortex, the limbic system and the hypothalamus. Activity of the cells in this part of the brain is directly or indirectly influenced by nerve fibres which fan out from a core region of the brain called reticular formation which reaches out to all the areas of the brain involved in regulating emotions. These activating fibres from the reticular formation must ascend or go upwards to reach the higher brain involved in emotion. The activating portion of the reticular formation is called the ascending reticular activating system (ARAS). The ARAS is fundamentally involved in keeping us awake, alert and conscious besides providing a tinge of arousal for emotional states.

Stress

Stress is an integral part of the natural fabric of life. Some of it occurs because we try to do too much in the time available and some because of difficulties with interpersonal relationships either at home or at work. Coping with stress and anxiety is needed for normal human growth and development. Any situation in which a person's behaviour is evaluated by others can be stressful, even the act of getting up in the morning generates enough stress. Going to school/college, being separated from parents or siblings, speaking or performing in public are among the many potential sources of stress.

Richard S. Lazarus, a leading authority on psychological stress, suggests that stress could be simply described as a special kind of transaction between a person and his environment. This view places equal emphasis upon the demands of the environment and the coping skills of the individual. In commonsensical terms, stress refers both to the circumstances that place physical or psychological demands on an individual and the emotional reactions experienced in these situations. Any change in the environment—even a pleasant one, such as a vacation—demands effort, like planning how to commute and reach that place, with whom to go and where to stay.

Many such small stresses and brief stress responses can add up to hundreds a day. These are parts of our life that we hardly notice and almost take for granted. If you work in an office, stress may accumulate with every ring of the phone and every meeting you squeeze into your already busy schedule. If you are a housewife, all the endless routine chores you must do can mount up just as quickly and take their toll as those faced in the office. For the city dweller, crowded living conditions are one of the most obvious and important sources of stress. Noise, traffic congestion and pollution are among the many by products of high population density. Unemployment, poverty, malnutrition and poor sanitary conditions are still generally associated with large cities.

The problems faced by the people may be different and unique to their own situations, but medical research has shown that in many respects the body responds in a stereotyped manner with identical biological changes, essentially meant to cope with any type of increased demand upon the human machinery. Psychological stress is currently defined in at least two different ways. It refers to the dangerous, potentially harmful or unpleasant external situations and, secondly, to the internal thoughts, judgements, emotional states and physiological processes that are evoked by stressful stimuli.

Events that act as stressors generally relate to one's status, one's power, one's territory and one's belief system. Disruption of such relationships leads to emotional response, eg., depression at loss of status, anger at invasion of one's territory and disgust at threats to one's beliefs. Man's ability to dwell over the past and anticipate the future may still be another source. In addition, distance is no longer a buffer. Mass media makes us instantly aware of wars, famine, political unrest, terrorism and economic chaos and frightening possibilities for the future.

The rate of change in our lives is accelerating. Alvin Toffler's *Future Shock* makes you realise that the unexpected has become a part of our day-to-day existence. These unexpected situations are some things we cannot overcome physically. But the extra chemical energy produced by our bodies in anticipation of the flight or fight response is not useful in most of the stressful situations in modern life because we have few physical battles to fight and almost nowhere to run. In the past, the demands for fulfilling one's basic needs for food, shelter and safety made good use of heightened arousal. None of these outlets are available any longer and it is clear that for life in the twentieth century, our emotional stress mechanisms are invariably unnecessary and harmful. Even if we could somehow 'burn off' all the chemicals produced by emotional states, psychological distress can interfere with productivity, learning, and interpersonal relationships, thereby upsetting us. If stress reactions increase, we become less adaptive. Our ability to understand and interact with other people is affected.

Factors involved in stress is one of the areas in which the interaction between situational, personal and biological factors is clearly seen.

Situational Factors

The nature of stressful circumstances affect our adjustment. The general effects of situational variation include the following.

- *Duration*
  An interview lasts a short while whereas repercussions of a quarrel might last for hours or days.
- *Severity*
  A minor injury is easier to tolerate than a major illness.
- *Predictability*
  The amount of stress resulting from having to perform in public might depend on whether you are prepared for it or not.
- *Controllability*
  One of the most upsetting aspects of a situation is the feeling that one is unable to exert any influence on the circumstances.

For example, victims of an earthquake can do little to stop the disaster.

- *Suddenness of onset*
  An accident may be difficult to cope with because it is completely unexpected, whereas challenges that can be foreseen may be easier to manage.

Biological Factors

When situational and personal factors combine to produce stress, our body responds in a characteristic manner. One of the world's foremost medical authorities on the effects of stress, Hans Selye (1956, 1976), proposed that bodily stress reactions follow a three-stage adaptation syndrome (GAS). The first stage is the *alarm reaction* which is essentially the emergency response of the body mediated by sympathetic nervous system. If the stress persists, the individual enters the second stage *resistance* during which the body recovers from the initial stress reaction and starts adapting to the situation. There is decreased output from the sympathetic nervous system, and increased output than the normal output from the adrenal cortex and the pituitary gland. The individual will eventually reach a final stage of *exhaustion* if the stress still continues.

Vulnerability to Stress

Some people are more vulnerable in all situations because they are generally less able to deal effectively with what happens to them in daily life. Other people are more vulnerable simply because of conditioning of unconnected events that have stressed them. A schoolgoing child may adapt better if he has a sympathetic teacher and when he is in good health but if he dislikes his teacher, is incapacitated, his not doing well in studies may upset him more than expected.

Stressors in themselves are neither good nor bad. They are simply events that either have a direct effect on the body or an indirect effect through various mediators. The bodily reactions to stressors are basically attempts at adaptation and if the stressors are not too extreme or too chronic, such attempts to adapt are usually successful. In that sense, stress reactions are good in that they are part of homeostatic mechanisms. If, however, the stressor becomes chronic, the ability of the body to successfully adapt is often compromised or the bodily response may have secondary undesirable consequences.

From still another point of view, some authors have suggested that psychological stressors, eg., marital conflicts or work demands, sometimes have the effect of improving coping skills, strengthening certain personality traits and increasing work productivity.

Some people deliberately expose themselves to various levels of stress, either through exercise or through exposure to dangerous situations, eg., hand gliding or auto racing.

Some people react to hard work and responsibility with worry and anxiety while the same amount and type of work can be challenging and rewarding for others. At first glance, it may seem that feelings of apprehension are emotional reactions to stressful situations as they are influenced by both the real potential dangers of those situations and the individual assessment of the situation.

Nevertheless, some situations are inherently more stressful than others, like injuries or infections of the body, annoying or dangerous events in our environment, major changes or transitions in life which force one to cope in new ways and in cases of anticipated or actual threats to one's self-esteem. When people interpret a stressful situation as dangerous or threatening, they also undergo physiological and behavioural changes resulting from the activation or arousal of the autonomic nervous system. The intensity of the reaction is proportional to the magnitude of the perceived danger or threat.

Stress Prevention by Teaching Coping Skills

The effectiveness of a stressor in influencing physical or mental illness depends on the coping resources available to each individual. Coping resources are of two kinds: internal and external. Internal resources refer to such coping skills as denial, displacement or substitution, and they may be learned haphazardly through the maturation process.

External resources refer to such things as financial supports and social network.

Pitchik (1980) suggested eight basic coping skills for dealing with problems of stressors that are related to ego defences
- Getting information
- Doing the opposite of what you feel
- Minimising the importance of the stressor
- Avoiding the stressor
- Seeking help
- Overcoming shortcomings
- Blaming others
- Doing unrelated pleasurable activities.

Stress inoculation is based on the idea that stress is achieved by exposing an individual to graded experiences of stress. Meichenbaum (1977) developed a procedure comprising the following components:
- Teaching individuals that negative self-evaluation and ruminations over decisions increase stress
- Monitoring one's own self-defeating strategies; teaching new cognitive strategies
- Teaching new skills, such as relaxation and better communication
- Providing real life homework assignments that become increasingly difficult to carry out

Relaxation Training

This approach to stress management has three forms. The first is concerned with simply teaching the individual how to relax using variations of Edmund Jacobson's Progressive Relaxation. The best known recent version of this is exemplified by the work of Benson and by his description of the relaxation response.

The second general approach to relaxation training is through some version of meditation or yoga. A third approach to relaxation training is through the use of bio-feedback. This method uses electronic instruments which provide overt, easily recognised information on the state of muscle tension. Such feedback is used by the individual to learn to reduce tension.

Still another technique designed to reduce stress is called *autogenic training*. It may be thought of as a variation of progressive relaxation and hypnosis and is based on auto-suggestion made by a person in the waking state.

Self-control
Self-control is the ability to control ourselves by being aware of and directing our actions to achieve specified goals (Karoly and Kanfer, 1982). The environment is not always under our control, but we may play an important role in how we respond to it.

Self-control implies self-direction. When people see themselves as having choices and perceive themselves as being in control, they are more likely to deal effectively with stress (Fisher, 1984). The mystery of a task-oriented technique lies not so much in "How do I feel?" but "What can I do?"

Part II
Yoga and the System and its Methodology

4
Classical Yoga

Yoga, based on ancient Indian wisdom and culture, is more than 5,000 years old and has been referred to by two specific words: *Sanatan*, which means eternal as the process of evolution and *Puratana*, meaning very ancient. The source of yoga resides in the *Vedas*, the *Upanishads*, the *Gita* and the *Sutras* of Patanjali. For centuries, countless millions throughout the world have used the systems and discipline of yoga for self-culture, self-evolution and self-realisation leading to immortality and freedom.

It was Rishi Patanjali, rightly called the Father of Yoga, who around 200 BC, compiled, synthesised, modified, systematised and refined yoga into a metaphysical whole, grafted on Samkhya philosophy and laid down eight steps which form the basis on which the whole system of yoga works. It was indeed the first classical attempt to interpret the subject. The eight steps consist of *Yama, Niyama, Asana, Pranayama, Pratyahara, Dharma, Dhyana* and *Samadhi*. These steps in perfect order, as they are, were formulated on the basis of a psychological understanding of the human mind. Yoga had recognised and accepted the importance of the mind and the subconscious over the total human personality much earlier than modern psychology did in its present form. In the methodology of Patanjali all the eight limbs or constituents are to be present in the same sequence with their correlation and ratios as recommended to make the process of yoga successful. Yoga, thus, is a stepwise, stagewise eightfold path to final liberation from pain and suffering.

These steps progressively take you to the highest state of creativity, of discriminative knowledge and towards attaining the desired perfection. There lies its great purpose and usefulness. There are some who emphasise only one or the other aspect of yoga, missing the integrated classical approach which alone can give total education for the transformation of the human personality from a disintegrated into an integrated one, sublimate man to divinity (from the ignoble to the noble). The classical yoga, commonly known as the *eightfold path* (Ashtanga Yoga), covers both the yoga ideology and technology.

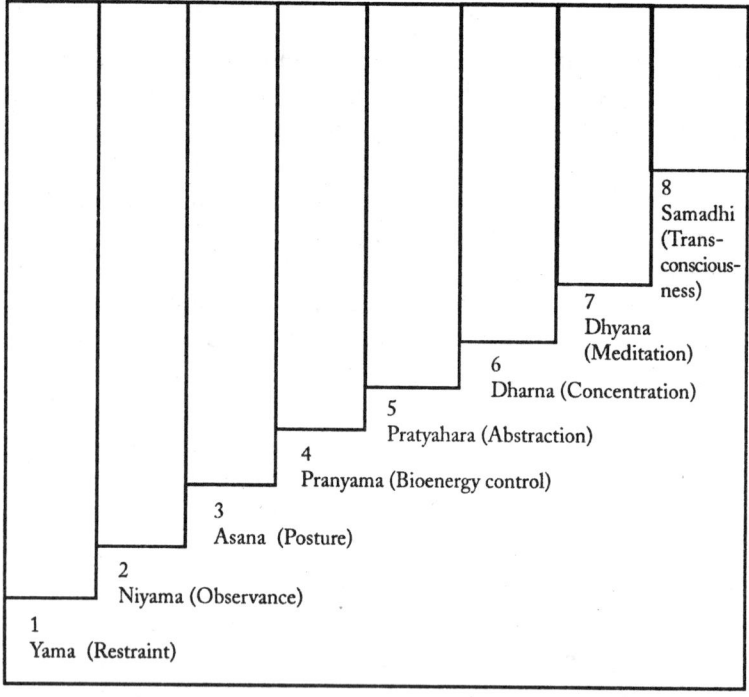

Fig 1

The eight steps are

Yama	-	Conditioned yoga behaviour, both personal and social.
Niyama	-	Attitudes sublimate to yoga norms.

Classical Yoga

Asana	-	Discipline of the physical body.
Pranayama	-	Control over bioenergy through respiratory action.
Pratyahara	-	Withdrawal of the senses inward through abstraction.
Dharna	-	Concentration.
Dhyana	-	Meditation
Samadhi	-	Absolute consciousness or transconsciousness (*Kaivalya*)

Of these, the first five, which border on the psychosomatic approach, are referred to as External (Bahiranga) Yoga, popularly known as Hatha Yoga, while the latter three, which directly affect the psyche are known as Internal (Antaranga) Yoga, popularly known as Raja Yoga. It is almost impossible to try Internal Yoga (Raja Yoga) for the average man before accomplishing the external one (Hatha Yoga).

Yoga is based on a deep understanding of man and his position in this world and was the first system evolved in the world to recognise the connection and the interaction between body and mind. It studies in depth the very structure of the human personality, thoroughly analyses the psychological complexities and the cause of human pain, sorrow and suffering. It has laid down psychosomatic means through its various psychophysiological processes for dealing with the body-mind complex and tries to harmonise and integrate the human personality at all levels and stages of life.

> ***Remember...***
> Yoga is basically a way of life which has been evolved as a system to go beyond the personality-complex and achieve absolute freedom (*Kaivalya*)—liberation of the soul from the matter.

5
Psychosomatic Approach to Yoga

In spite of the amazing progress in the field of science and technology, it is now being gradually realised by the great thinkers of the world in general and those of the West in particular, that man's problems have multiplied several-fold. This has resulted in abnormality, tension, anxiety, boredom and unhappiness. It is said that the present era is an Age of Anxiety—the commonest from of psychoneurosis. There is a wide spectrum of anxiety in states of tension including psychosomatic and organic illness. Stress arises out of tension and tension can be muscular, mental or emotional, creating an imbalance in the nervous system. Muscular tension is not difficult to eliminate and can be easily worked out by a sensible diet and proper rest. Mental tension is due to our wrong way of thinking and living; emotional tension arise from how we react to persons, objects and events in life. They say it is the emotional effect caused by the stress and strain of modern living which is expressed in so many psychosomatic diseases or stress related diseases. Emotional stress can cause distressing symptoms. Emotions can upset glandular functions, metabolic balance and also cause stomach disorders. There is a growing awareness of the importance of emotional factors involved in the activities and efficiency of the heart and the circulatory system. All tense reactions really depend on our personality, temperament, emotional stability and attitude which ultimately determine our Stress Threshold.

Yoga therefore tries to re-educate the patient to alter his Habitual Reaction Pattern, develop a coping mechanism and thus holds the key to better living. Yoga has laid down psychosomatic means through various psychophysiological processes for dealing with the body-mind complex and tries to harmonise and integrate the human personality at all levels and stages of life.

In the simplest of ways, emphasis is laid on two important aspects of *chitta* (personality-complex): Purity and achievement of mental poise and emotional stability.

According to Shri Yogendraji, "The impure, diffused, distracted and disintegrated mind is a great personal impediment standing in the way of individual and social well-being". Let us examine the psychosomatic approach. External (Bahiranga) Yoga—the first five steps of the eightfold path—comprise:

Yamaniyama (The First Two Steps)

Five Yamas

Conditioned yoga behaviour is to be practised in thoughts, words and deeds.

According to yoga, these five yamas guard us against the pitfalls that are to be avoided, and it is at every stage of impulse (*pratyaya*), when the individual is about to think, feel, speak or act that yoga takes charges and asks you to restrain thinking, speaking or acting in a manner that would create complications.

Restraint is the gateway to yoga.

The five yamas are:
- *Ahimsa* (Non-violence)
  Don't injure or hurt others. Avoid any tendency to violence, not only in action and speech but also in thought.
- *Satya* (Truth)
  Do not speak untruth. Think, speak and act nothing but truth.
- *Asteya* (Non-stealing)
  Put into practice the spirit of live and let live.
- *Brahmacharya* (Non-indulgence in sex)
  Discipline your sex life to purity and moderation to conform to marital obligations.
- *Aparigrah* (Non-covetousness)
  Accept your dues but expect no more.

Five Niyamas
The five niyamas are:
- *Savca* (Absolute purity)
  Keep your body and mind pure.
- *Santosha* (Contentment)
  Be content with what you have.
- *Tapa* (Fortitude)
  Cultivate fortitude so as to be indifferent to the pair of the opposites, like pleasure and pain, love and hatred, etc.
- *Svadhyaya* (Self-study)
  Pursue knowledge for self-evolution.
- *Ishvarapranidhana* (Resignation to the will of the Absolute).
  Discharge your duties honourably and leave the rest to the Absolute.

Asanas
The postural training programme of therapeutic asanas, its many characteristics of non-violent and non-fatiguing types, as evolved at the Yoga Institute, Mumbai, has a complete approach and therefore facilitates the correct interrelationship between the psychosomatic and the somato-psychic, for the well-being of human organism. Your mind then is free from bodily tension, discomfort and disease.

Pranayama
The yogic method of harmonious and deep breathing brings about a sedative effect on the nerves and you achieve mental equilibrium. Shri Yogendraji says, "Control of prana creates a mental condition of steadiness, thus allowing the growth of discriminative knowledge."

Pratyahara or Abstraction
The psychosomatic practices of yoga bring about a state of neuromuscular relaxation and increase the energy content as well, thereby helping the *sadhaka* to restrain his mind from all types of disctractions which leads to abstraction. Practices of meditation

act as a quietening process that calms the mind and helps you to acquire serenity of mind—a state of tranquillity.

Dharma, Dhyana and Samadhi
These take you to the higher aspect of Raja Yoga referred to as *samyama* which begins with concentration and ends with Absolute Consciousness.

Part III
Integrated Health Care Programme

6
Ill Health means Disharmony

In yoga, diseases are placed in three categories:
- *Bhautika* or physiological
- *Adhi Bhautika* or psychological
- *Adhyatimika* or psychic

But all these are interrelated—a fact which is very rarely understood or appreciated by the modern physician. According to the ideology of yoga, man lives not compartmentally, but at various levels—physical, mental, moral and spiritual simultaneously. Basically, we have to understand that ill health means some kind of disharmony in the living organism leading to a functional imbalance. The homeostat mechanism is disturbed. The upsetting of the functional integrity of the body is expressed in many somatic symptoms. There is a long chain of misalignment, maladjustment and malfunctioning in the various interrelated components (*koshas*) of the body, causing disharmony (*vighna*). All these have to be adjusted to the point of integrated harmony like the tuning of a radio set. Instant relief or symptomatic relief therefore has no meaning, since yoga thinks that the process of nature takes its own time to re-establish the normalcy of homeostasis.

Yoga therapy is based on four important concepts of *Ahar* (diet), *Achar* (relationship or code of conduct), *Vichar* (thought process) and *Vihar* (a balanced programme to handle the body-mind complex, rest and recreation). This holistic approach restores balance and brings about that harmony between body, mind and soul which provides relief and a cure for disease when a new yogic attitude and a way of life is applied, accepted and followed.

Causes of Tension
- Negative thoughts and attitudes.
- Lifestyle and habit structure.
- Temperament, disposition, tendencies and personality traits.
- Attachment to the ego; seeking pleasure and avoiding pain.
- Lack of faith in the Higher Reality.

7
Handling the Body-Mind Complex

Integrated Health Care Programme (A Basic Course)

In our health care programme, an integrated approach is adopted in which four distinct elements of Yoga are employed in a balanced way to deal with the body-mind complex. These are:
- Simple meditative postures (static asanas)
- Therapeutic rhythmical exercises (dynamic asanas)
- Breathing process (simplified pranayamas)
- Psychosomatic practices (total relaxation and meditation)

8
The Preparation and Conditioning of the Mind

In any systematic study of yoga, a certain amount of preparation is needed and so it is then that you follow this integral course.

One of the important objectives to be achieved in this course is to quieten and calm the mind. Most of the time the mind is not at rest. It wanders a lot and is easily distracted. There may be conflicting ideas or thoughts, or you may be emotionally upset. To get rid of all this agitation of the mind, you have to make an attempt to compose the mind through a process of *conditioning*. Therefore, a proper mental framework is created by way of inwardness. Your mind too is quietened and you are more receptive. You have the right frame of mind for any activity that follows or you take up. The central idea of learning meditative postures is to see whether we can withdraw our attention from the outside world and localise it to our body and its subtle working. It leads to a deeper awareness of one's body-mind complex. It is the first positive step to develop a subjective process of inwardness.

Instructions on Meditative Postures
During this practice the attention should shift to different parts of the body—head and neck, keeping the spine erect, the abdomen drawn in a little and not allowing it to relax or protrude, the arms relaxed with no tension at elbow joints, the shoulders drawn a little backwards, the palms on the knees. After keeping the mind busy for some time in this way, the next important thing is to attend to

The Preparation and Conditioning of the Mind

the act of breathing. We just simply watch the inhalation and the exhalation that is going on. If we can continue this very simple exercise with our eyes closed for a short while, watching passively our own breathing rhythm, the rhythm and harmony of this action can create a peaceful feeling and lead to tranquillity.

Don't fight with the mind or try to suppress any thought or force yourself to drive out the thoughts. With your passive attitude you can watch the flow of thoughts and slowly bring your mind to a smaller area of breathing.

Application

For elimination of nervous agitation, attainment of composure, ease in breathing and concentration. Practise before starting your daily yoga routine practice.

The meditative postures are:

Sukhasana (The Easy Posture)

Fig 2

Posture
Siting in a cross-legged position with heels below the thighs and keeping the spine erect (Fig 2).

Methods
- Sit with legs crossed at the ankles.
- Place heels comfortably below the thighs.
- Place palms on knees, and keep elbows relaxed.
- Keep spine erect, and head and neck straight.
- Draw abdomen in normal contour.
- Close your eyes and mentally go through earlier instructions.
- Maintain normal breathing.
- Remind yourself to be quiet as and when other thoughts try to force their way in.

Rhythm
Normal breathing.

Duration
7-10 minutes.

Benefits
Corrects postural defects, loosens lower joints, provides fixity of base, promotes favourable circulatory changes and also changes in respiratory rate and pulse rate, leads to mental conditioning, and acts as a preparatory step to meditation.

Vajrasana (The Adamant Posture): A meditative posture

Posture
In kneeling position with upturned feet, place the buttocks in the cavity formed by keeping heels apart and maintain the spine erect (Fig 3).

Method
- Sit in a kneeling position.
- Slip toes to join at the back, keeping the heels apart and the big toes pointed towards each other.
- Place buttocks in the cavity thus formed, keeping thighs together.

The Preparation and Conditioning of the Mind

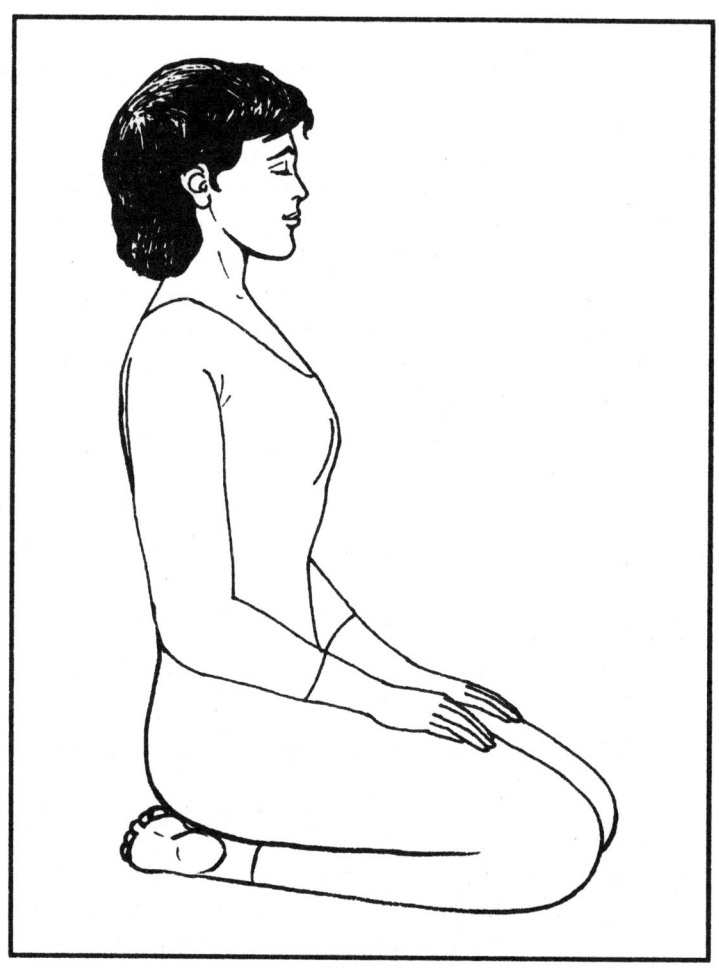

Fig 3

- Adjust the hands on respective thighs, keeping the spine erect, and head and neck straight.
- Draw abdomen in contour.
- Close your eyes and mentally go through the earlier instructions.
- Maintain normal breathing.
- Remind yourself to be quiet as and when other thoughts force their way in.

Note: If there is pain in the ankles or a feeling of discomfort beyond your endurance (usual in the early stages of practice), use a soft cushion or fold your towel and place it under your feet. Gradually increase the duration of the practice from 3 minutes to 10 minutes. The great advantage of *Vajrasana* is that it keeps the spine erect and in a very correct position automatically. Any stiffness in the ankle-joints will disappear after practising for a week or so.

Rhythm
Normal breathing.

Duration
5-7 minutes.

Benefits
Corrects posture, better flexion of ankle and feet, relaxation of thigh muscles, good fixity, helps in digestion and breathing, gives relief in backache, mental conditioning, a preparatory step to meditation.

Remember...
- Do not slouch; keep the spine erect.
  If you find difficulty in maintaining the spine erect in *Sukhasana*, take the support of a wall for your back.
- In case *Vajrasana* is too painful, use a cushion under your ankles.
- Do not interfere with your natural breathing.
- Do not let your attention wander from your breathing.

9
Restore Balance and Rhythm for Inner Harmony

Health is the Outer Expression of a Deep Harmony
Shri Yogendraji says, "All the parts maintain their level of efficiency when in use and lose their function when not in use—this is a biological fundamental."

Nature follows the laws of balance, rhythm and harmony. The wear and tear of our body is compensated by nature during sleep at night. This helps in maintaining the steady rhythm of life. In this way efficiency is maintained at the level of the body and the mind. Similarly the recreating process (quiet entertainment) is a means to recreate the body and the mind which has lost something. To maintain the balance one has to regain it—hence such short breaks at intervals when properly blended with activity will result in better health. In the training programme for yoga postures, rhythmical exercises are to be treated as a complete body phenomenon in which poise and balance are maintained at all times and the attention is fixed unwaveringly on the movements being executed. Asanas therefore are attitude bound to achieve a unison of body and mind and to contribute to steadiness and comfort (*Sthir Sukhasanam*).

10
The Basic Ideal

Our mental perspective is distorted by nervous tension. In all yoga exercises and processes, the main stress is on the growth, development and purification of the nervous system (*Nadi Shuddhi*) which affects not only the various internal organs purposefully but also tends towards poise and mental health. It facilitates a harmonious body-mind relationship by proper coordination, balance and neuro-muscular control.

Method

These are static-cum-dynamic variations of asanas based on the principle of relaxation. If there is stiffness in key points of your body, especially in the muscles, ligaments and joints, there is need for a gentle stretching movement and proper rhythm for the release of tension from muscular and nervous strain. These therapeutic rhythmical exercises are performed with slow movements with a brief holding (static pause) which we effectively utilise as a pause of retention (inspiratory standstill) or suspension (expiratory standstill). It is important to note that breathing should be ideally coordinated with body movement to achieve perfect synchronisation and that a rhythm is maintained. In short, all these act as a series of coordinated phases with alternate stretching and relaxation of the muscles, providing the necessary stimulation which is organically vital to improve your blood circulation, relieve muscle spasms, revitalise and rejuvenate all your internal organs so as to yield maximum well-being. They are non-violent and non-fatiguing type of practices to suit all age-groups. There is ease and grace in movement and perfect economy of means—the process being anabolic.

Two important areas in the trunk are emphasised: the spine and the abdomen. Besides, the exercises affect the nerve centres that control the muscles of the trunk to increase the health and efficiency of the nervous system. We have carefully selected only six therapeutic asanas. Three in a standing, two in a sitting, and one in a lying down position.

11
Guidelines for Performance

All the six therapeutic asanas are to be treated as a slow series of rhythmic movements accompanied by either inhalation or exhalation with a short static pause of 3 seconds of retention or suspension as prescribed. Gradually, increase this pause period from three to a maximum of six seconds in two months time in each of the asanas to derive maximum benefit. The final ratio of Yogendra breathing rhythm will be 3:6:3. The movements have to be slow, free from vigorous effort and strain. Avoid any unnecessary pulls of muscles so that antagonistic muscles are relaxed at the proper time and thus do not impede the functioning of the acting muscles. It reduces tension and fatigue.

12
Therapeutic Postures

The following are the therapeutic postures that release tension by gentle stretching and coordination.

Talasana (The Palm Posture) and its two variations.

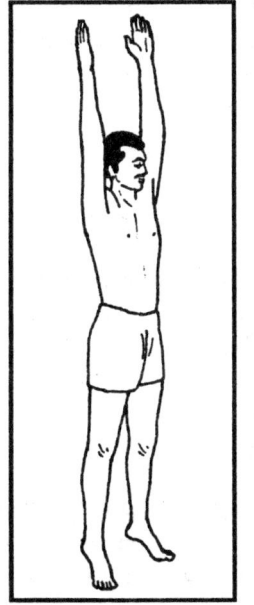 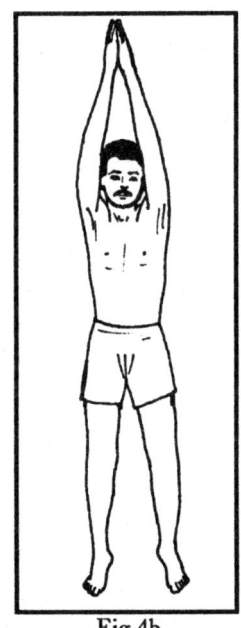

Fig 4a Fig 4b

(a) First variation (Fig 4a)
Methods
- Stand straight, with feet a hand-span apart, and parallel; arms alongside the body.

- Maintain an erect spine and head.
- Focus attention on a spot at the level of your eyes.
- Breathing in, simultaneously raise the heels and the arms forwards and upwards, palms facing inwards.
- On reaching the maximum stretch position, maintain it and hold the breath.
- Breathing out, simultaneously bring down the heel and the arms sideways, palms facing downwards.
- Pause and repeat.

Duration
The movement has to be repeated 6 times.

Breathing Rhythm
Breathing in/upward movement: 3 seconds.
Holding the breath/maintaining maximum stretch: 3 seconds
Breathing out/downward movement: 3 seconds.
Suspending the breath/pause: 3 seconds.

Note: As your proficiency in the asana increases, raise the time of holding the breath up to 6 seconds.

(b) Second variation (Fig 4b)
- Do exactly as above, but raise both the arms from sideways and upwards, palms facing upwards, till they meet over the head in a maximum stretch position. The movement has to be repeated 6 times with a brief pause of holding the breath for 3 seconds when maintaining maximum stretch.

Benefits
Stretches the entire body; the rhythmic breathing helps in the expansion of the lungs and develops respiratory muscles, exercises and massages the abdominal viscera indirectly, increases height (up to a certain age) and gives vertical stretch to the spine. It increases neuro-muscular coordination.

Konasana (The Angle Pose)
Method
- Stand comfortably, with feet about 3 hand-spans apart and parallel.

Therapeutic Postures

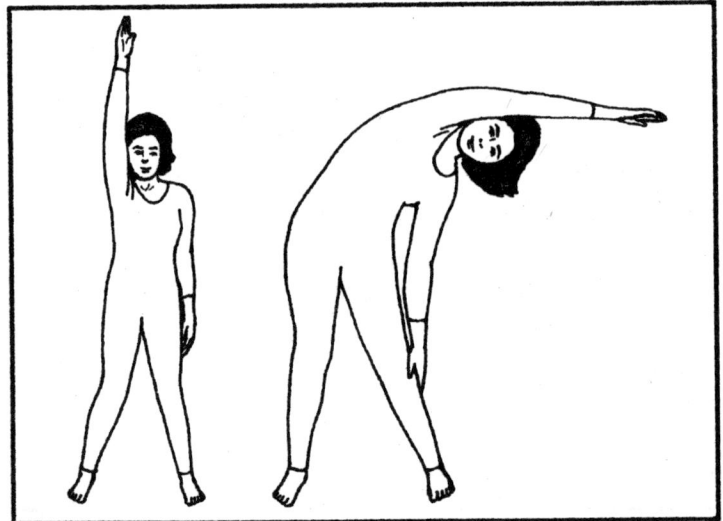

Fig 5

- Raise the right arm, making contact between the arm and the ear.
- Breathing in, and without bending your knees, bend sideways to the left simultaneously sliding the left hand down your leg.
- Holding your breath, maintain the maximum stretch position.
- Breathing out, return to the standing position.
- Suspending the breath, simultaneously bring down the right arm and raise the left.
- Repeat on the other side.

Duration
3 rounds—each round consisting of alternate bending, first to the right and then to the left.

Breathing Rhythm
Suspension of breath/raising the arms: 3 seconds
Breathing in/sideways bending: 3 seconds.
Holding the breath/maintaining maximum stretch position: 3 seconds.

Note: As your proficiency in the asana increases, raise the time of holding the breath up to 6 seconds.

Benefits
Provides lateral stretch to the spine; exercises the less used muscles of the sides and waist; compresses and massages the body organs like the liver, stomach, kidneys, large intestine, etc.; removes fat and obesity.

Trikonasana (Triangle Posture)

Method
- Stand erect keeping the feet together; raise your hands over your head and breathe in.
- While breathing out, bend the body forward from above the waist.
- Try to touch the toes with fingers without bending the knees and maintain the position with the suspension of breath.

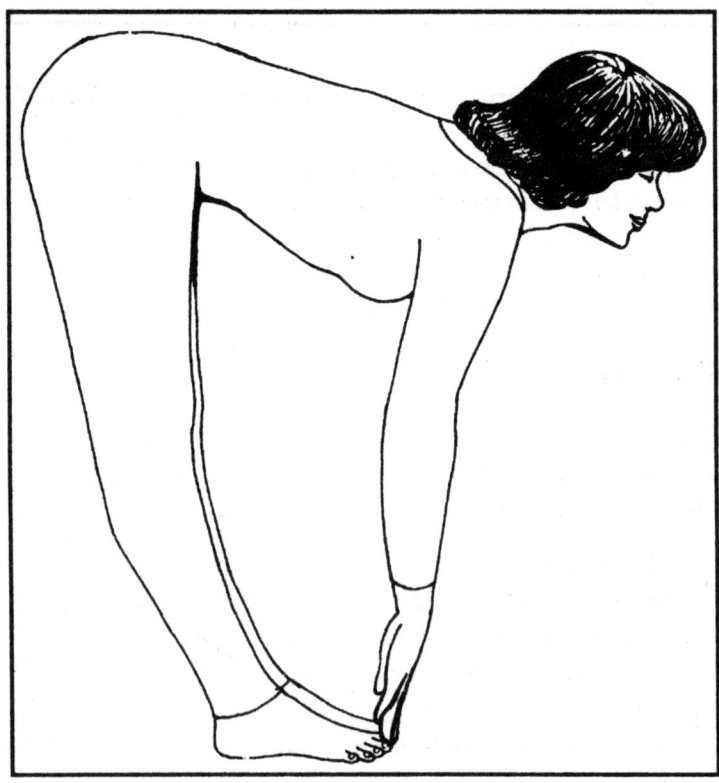

Fig 6

- Breathing in, return to original position.

Note: Keep one hand-span distance between the feet and bend forward slowly from the waist, keeping the head downwards. Give a gentle downward pressure but don't bend the knees. As flexibility improves, the fingers may touch the ground. Then perform it as mentioned above.

Duration
Repeat five times.

Breathing Rhythm
Breathing out/bending forward movement: 3 seconds.
Suspending the breath/pause: 3 seconds.
Breathing in/return to original position: 3 seconds.

Benefits
Posterior stretching of the spine; increase in flexibility of the waist; exercises the hips; stretching of the muscles of the legs and arms; hamstring muscles are strengthened; good effect on the sciatic nerve; corrects faulty posture-habits by intra-abdominal compression.

Vakrasana (The Spinal Twist)

Method
- Sit with your legs outstretched, legs and feet touching.
- Rest your hands lightly on your thighs.

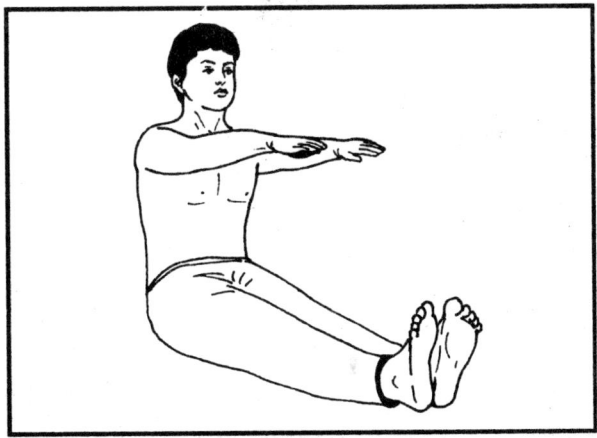

Fig 7a

- Breathing in, raise your arms to shoulder level (Fig 7a).
- Breathing out, swing both the arms and the upper part of the body, the neck and the head to the right (Fig 7b).
- Breathing in, return to the starting position maintaining your arms at shoulder level.
- Repeat, twisting to the left.
- Breathing in, return to the starting position.
- Breathing out, drop the hands back to the thighs.
- Pause for a while.
- Breathing in, raise your arms once again to shoulder level.

Duration
5 rounds — each round consisting of alternate twisting, once to the right and once to the left.

Breathing Rhythm
- Breathing in/raising the arms: 3 seconds.
- Breathing out/twisting (to right) : 3 seconds.
- Breathing in/untwisting: 3 seconds.
- Breathing out/twisting (to left): 3 seconds.
- Breathing in/untwisting: 3 seconds.

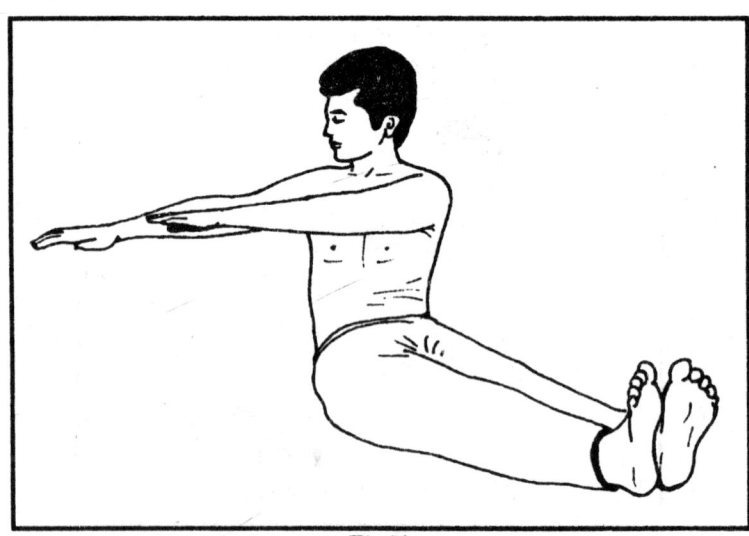

Fig 7b

- Breathing out/dropping the hands: 3 seconds.
- Pause of suspension/no movement: 3 seconds.

Benefits
Gives a gentle twist to the spine, removes obesity; removal of minor displacements of vertebrae.

Note: Do not raise or hunch your shoulders.

Yoga Mudra (The Symbol of Yoga)

Method
- Sit in *Sukhasana*.
- Taking the arms behind the back, hold the left wrist with the right hand and clench the left fist.
- Breathing in, pull the hands as far up as possible, behind the back.
- Holding the breath, twist the torso to the right.
- Breathing out, simultaneously bring down the head to touch the right knee and relax the arms by sliding the hands down.
- Suspend the breath and maintain this position.

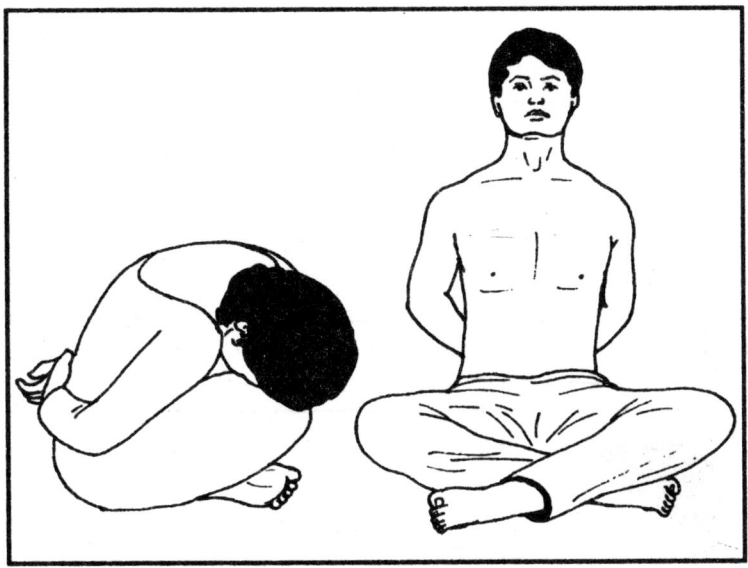

Fig 8

- Breathing in, simultaneously raise the torso and pull the hands up against the back.
- Repeat, bending forward to touch the floor between the knees with your forehead.

Duration
3 rounds — each round consisting of alternate twisting and bending—once to the right, once to the left and, finally, bending once at the centre.

Yoga mudra is contra-indicated during the first 3 days of menstruation and also in case of high blood pressure.

Breathing Rhythm
- Breathing in/raising hands up against the back: 3 seconds.
- Holding the breath/twisting the torso: 3 seconds.
- Breathing out/bending and sliding: 3 seconds.
- Suspending the breath/maintaining position: 3 seconds.
- Breathing in/raising torso and pulling up hands: 3 seconds.

Benefits
Posterior stretching of the spine; lateral stretching of almost all the posterior muscles of the trunk and neck; intra-abdominal compression giving a gentle massage to the internal organs; improves circulation of blood in the face and head regions; improves elimination of toxic wastes; leads to a relaxed, passive state of consciousness.

Bhujangasana (The Snake Posture)

Method
- Lie on your abdomen with your legs stretched and toes pointing outwards and rest your palms below the shoulders, touching your nose lightly on the ground (Fig 9a).

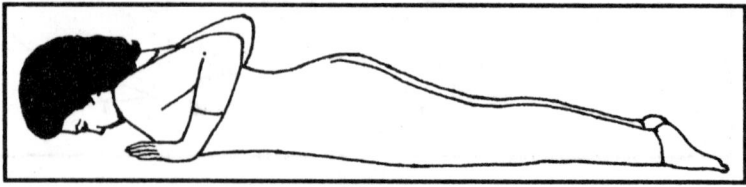

Fig 9a

- Breathing in, and lightly pressing the floor with your palms, slowly raise and curve back your head, neck and upper torso (Fig 9b).

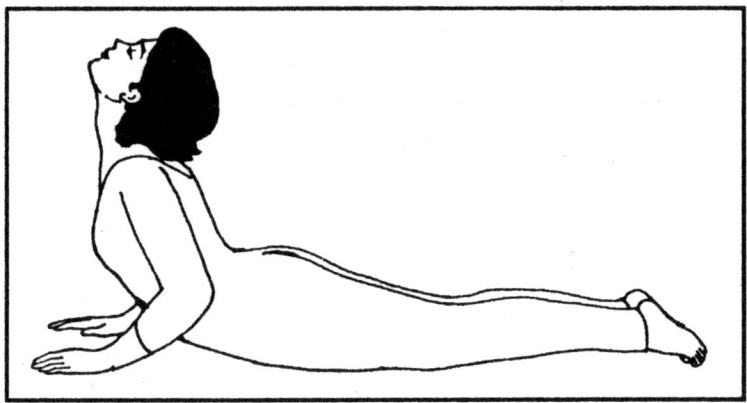

Fig 9b

- Hold your breath and maintain this position.
- Breathing out, gently lower yourself back to the floor.
- Breathing normally, turn the head sideways and relax the body.

Duration
5 times

Breathing Rhythm
- Breathing in/curving the torso upwards and backwards: 3 seconds.
- Holding the breath/maintaining the position: 3 seconds.
- Breathing out/lowering the body: 3 seconds.

Benefits
Adjusts minor displacements of the vertebrae; exercises and tones the deep muscles supporting the spinal column and the trunk; promotes spinal circulation; provides relief from flatulence and abdominal adhesions; relieves backache.

Note: Do not raise the portion of the body which is below the navel. Contra-indicated during mensuration and advanced pregnancy, hernia and colitis.

Remember...
- Never strain or force yourself to achieve an extreme position—just go as far as you can in backward and forward bending.
- Remember these rhythmical exercises are to be performed with:
  — Coordinated breathing
  — Correct technique
  — Precision
  — Will power
  In this manner, asanas become attitude bound.
- You should be totally involved in the activity of the moment by coordinating your mind with the body and by your total presence. Make good use of this habit in each and every act during the day (general application).
- Also observe the interfering tension that comes in the body when you suffer from the stresses and strains of daily life.

13
Simplified Pranayamas
(Breathing Process)

All life exists only from breath to breath
— Shri Yogendraji

Long and deep breathing has a sedative effect on the nerves.

Pranayama is the fourth step in the systematic study of Yoga. Its full significance has to be properly understood and appreciated. It consists of two components; *Pran + ayama*. *Prana* is translated by Shri Yogendraji as bioenergy and *Ayama* means control of bioenergy. *Prana* is life-force, an essential living agent that works in the human body and makes its various functions possible.

Prana is supplied by food, air and solar energy. It is manifested in different forms—when it flows in the nerves it is called nervous energy; in the muscles it is muscular energy; in the seminal fluid it is sexual energy. In its finer form it becomes mental power, thought power, power of imagination, etc. Hence, energies of the vital life-force are discharged through the nervous system containing 72,000 nerves or nadis through *Prana Vahaka* or nerve impulses. Raja Yoga reminds us that mind and body together has only one life-force. *Prana* also is a cosmic phenomenon. The ancient yogis thought about it, not only as a physical reality, but also as a universal reality— as the world energy principle, pervading and sustaining life.

Yogis mobilise this energy and use it to heal any desired part of the body. *Prana* is not *vayu* or breath but since outside us it is surcharged with maximum energy, all importance is given to the yogic method of deep breathing. One can absorb larger quantities of atmospheric energy in this way. But how can one do this unless one has learnt to expand the lungs to one's fullest capacity from the apex to the base? Remember, unless your breathing is full and steady, your nervous system is bound to be adversely affected. In any problem of health, prime consideration must be given to breathing—the basic root of existence.

14
Yogic Complete Breath

To utilise the lungs to their full capacity, it is important to train the three sets of respiratory muscles: (a) the diaphragm, (b) the intercostal muscles, and (c) the clavicular muscles (muscles around the armpit and collar bone). When all these three respiratory muscles coordinate well, the bony cage of ribs opens up well, the diaphragm descends down, the chest cavity is enlarged allowing the lungs to take in oxygen to its full capacity and the objective of complete breath is achieved. All this development is needed for hyperoxygenation, thereby helping the brain function with clear blood and also as a reserve of oxygen. This is a good investment against diseases like pleurisy, pneumonia, T.B. and other respiratory troubles. Remember, blood with a low oxygen content is open to disease.

A simple system of preliminary pranayamas has been evolved by Shri Yogendraji whereby the respiratory mechanism is fully harmonised and organically developed which also leads to regulation and control of respiratory movements. All this is very easy, safe and useful to the modern man. Yogendra pranayama No. 1 is a conditioning process to establish harmony at the respiratory level. Numbers 2, 3 and 4 are specific methods of breathing to give exercise to a particular set of respiratory muscles. In course of time, you will be able to coordinate all the respiratory muscles for a yogic complete breath. Breathing through alternate nostrils is also included to regulate the varied effects of breath on the body and the mind.

15
Pranayama Practices can Help in Many Ways

- To develop the respiratory organs and to improve your vital capacity (lung capacity).
- To aid the circulation of the blood.
- To produce inner, organic and natural harmony.
- To provide efficient control over the respiratory movements.
- Long and deep breathing produces a sedative effect on nerves.
- Useful for emotional control.
- Helps in steadiness of the mind and in concentration.
- More bioenergy (*prana*) is absorbed and stored in the body.
- Preparation for meditation takes place when breathing becomes subtle.

16
General Precautions

- Breathe in and breathe out through the nose only.
- Do it without producing any sound.
- Relax your body and keep your mind calm before commencing pranayama. Do it as indicated in the guide table or after *savasana*.
- Keep a count of time by uttering numbers mentally; equalise your breathing in and breathing out.
- Do it in the morning and in the evening—twice a day is sufficient. To progress, add one count every week to reach to a maximum of 8 or 10 seconds in each inhalation/exhalation.
- Take a few normal breaths after each type of pranayama and generally start with slow exhalation.
- Practise not more than three types of pranayamas in one sitting and do not exceed the total of thirty rounds—ten rounds in each pranayama.
- Concentrate on your breathing. It is very important to do it smoothly, gently without strain. Try to acquire a steady control over your respiratory movements. It should be a uniform, continuous movement—both inhalation and exhalation—without a pause of retention or suspension.

17
Create Rhythm of Breath to Harmonise Thoughts

Breathing is directly related to your mental thought conditions and emotional life. When you are angry, your breath is fast, jerky, uneven and short, and when your are calm and tranquil, watch your breath and you will find that it is smooth, even and rhythmic. Breathing indicates emotional instability or mental agitation or disturbance, specially through rhythms. The reverse is also true. By controlling our flow and by harmonious and rhythmic breathing you can bring about mental equilibrium and quieten your mind—your anxiety and tension are dissolved. Your power of concentration improves with much less disturbance and distraction. By learning Yogendra Pranayama No. 1, you create harmony at the respiratory level.

Yogendra Pranayama No. 1 (In standing or sitting position)
For Conditoning Process (A simple form of Ujjayi)
- To put your attention on the normal flow of breathing.
- To give a feeling of ease in practice.
- To make you time-conscious.
- To acquire a gentle control over the respiratory movements and gradually to prolong the act of respiration.

Method
- Stand erect in a relaxed manner with feet apart.
- Inhale slowly, comfortably and smoothly in a continuous manner for 4 seconds.

- At the end of each inhalation, start exhaling with the same speed of inhalation—4 seconds, ie., equalise inhalation and exhalation timings.
- Let there be no jerks or strain. Do it effortlessly and concentrate on the uninterrupted flow of breath.

Frequency
Repeat 10 rounds starting with your easy count which you should be able to maintain. Gradually increase by one count every week and come to a count of 10 seconds.

Note: Keep timing either by looking at the watch or mentally counting "one-thousand-one", "one-thousand-two", etc., or counting numbers mentally at the same speed. Later, this practice can be done sitting in a meditative posture.

Benefits
Better oxygenation; even use of inspiratory and expiratory effort; sense of harmony; improved concentration.

Yogendra Pranayama No. 2 (In standing position)
(Intercostal Breathing or Rib Breathing)

Method
- Assume standing position as in Pranayama No. 1.
- Place your hands on the lower portion of the ribs on either side as shown in Fig 10a.

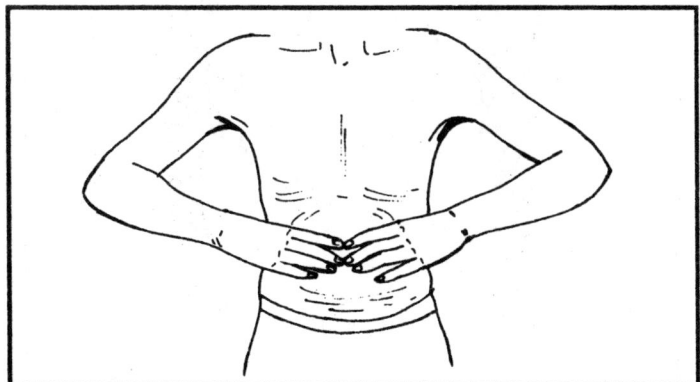

Fig 10a

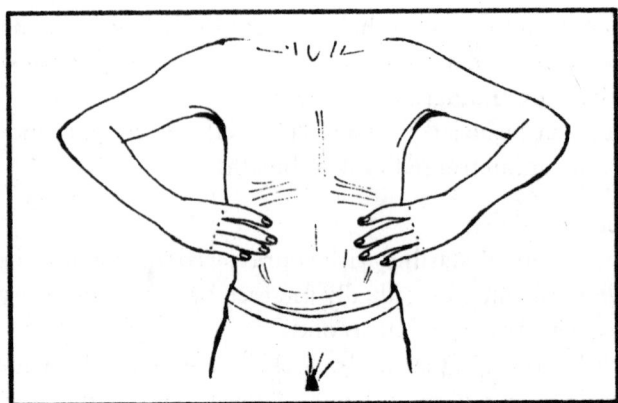

Fig 10b

- Now inhale in such a way that the lateral movement of the ribs is distinctly felt (Fig 10b), by expanding the intercostal muscles—muscles in between the ribs (Fig 10c). Do it to a count of five to manage easily.

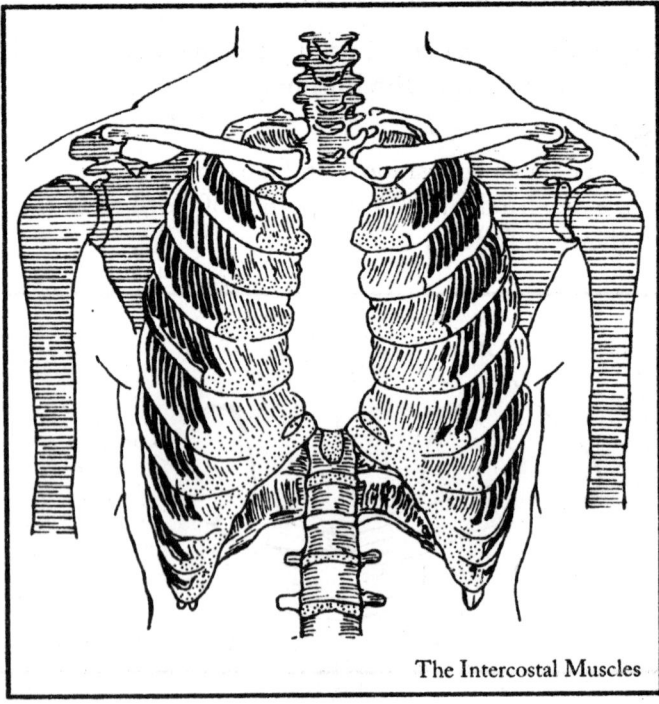

The Intercostal Muscles

Fig 10c

- Start exhalation soon after inhalation is complete, to the same count of five seconds and feel the gradual inflation of the ribs—the lateral movement of the ribs can be distinctly felt.
- See that the abdomen is held in normal contour and there is no vertical movement of the bony cage.
- Note that in every round you equalise your inhalation and exhalation to a count of five.

Frequency
Repeat up to 10 rounds. Gradually add one count every week after starting with five initially.

Note: Do not attempt to increase the counts or the rounds to ten.

Benefits
Improves control of intercostal muscles; increases ventilation, especially the lower lobes of the lungs get activated; increases vital capacity; general contour of the chest improves.

Yogendra Pranayama No. 3 (In standing position)
(Clavicular Breathing)

Method
- Assume a relaxed standing position.
- After normal exhalation, begin to inhale gently upwards, concentrating on the vertical movement of the upper chest.
- Raise the shoulders slowly upwards and restrict the count to 4 or 6 seconds to start with.
- Without any retention of breath, slowly exhale. Equalise the inhalation and exhalation timings.
- During the whole process keep the abdomen and the lower part of the ribs under control—the attention should be on the upper chest region and the area below the armpits. Breathing should be smooth without any jerks or strain.

Frequency
Repeat 10 rounds—start with your easy count and gradually add one count every week and reach a count of 10 seconds.

Benefits

Accessory muscles are used; ventilation of the apex of lungs is improved and both *puraka* (inspiration) and *rechaka* (expiration) are deepened; brings about increase in vital capacity.

Yogendra Pranayama No. 4 (In lying down position) (Diaphragmatic Breathing)

Method

- Lie supine and bend legs at knees, keeping the soles of the feet on the ground.
- Place one hand on the abdomen and the other hand on the side. Relax the abdomen.
- With inhalation, allow the abdomen to rise up, but not too much.

Diaphragm

An important muscle in breathing, separating the abdomen from the thoracic cavity.

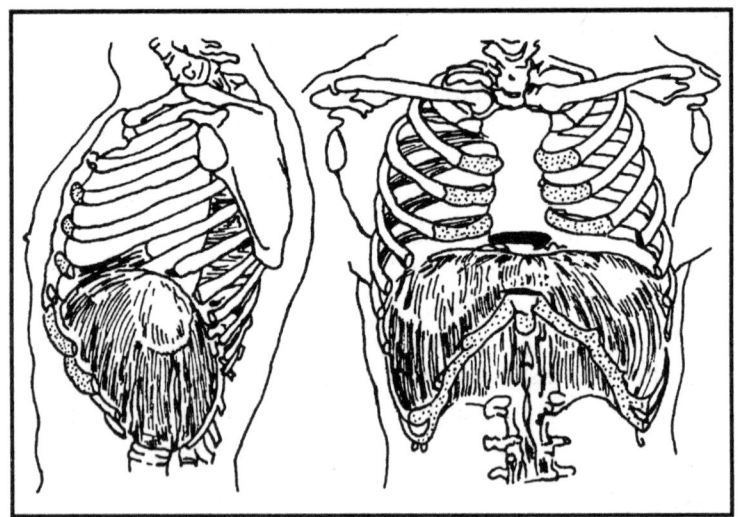

Fig 11a The Diaphragm A—Tendon

With inspiration it contracts, flattening out downward and with expiration it is restored to its relaxed dome-shaped position.

- With exhalation, allow the abdomen to descend (Fig 11c).
- Keep a count and equalise the timing of inhalation and exhalation.
- Allow the counts to remain at five in the beginning.

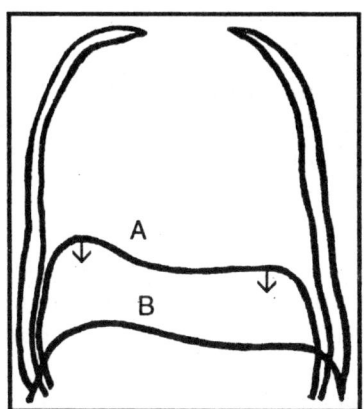

Fig 11b Action of the Diaphragm A. Expiration B.Inspiration

Frequency
Repeat 10 to 15 rounds—start with your easy count of five and gradually increase it to 8 seconds.

Benefits
Exercises the abdomen and the diaphragm. Provides relief from respiratory troubles, cures constipation, reduces obesity and aids relaxation.

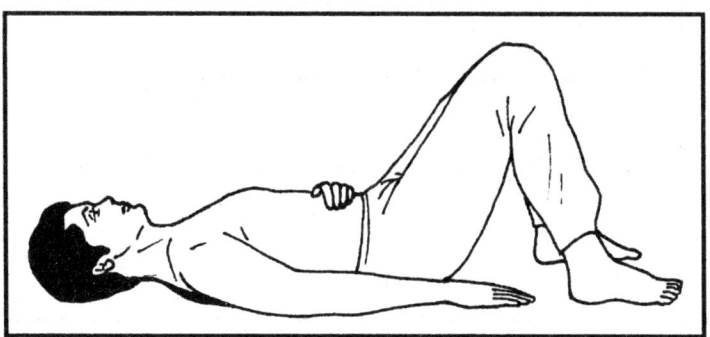

Fig 11c

Note: Later, practise Yogendra Pranayama No. 4 in sitting position in a meditative posture.

The Yogic Complete Breath (In sitting position)

As a process of preparatory *pranayamas*, we have learnt three distinct types of breathing. This is mainly to focus on and to provide exercise separately to three sets of respiratory muscles, viz:
- Abdominal or diaphragmatic breathing — Y. P. No. 4
- Intercostal or 'rib' breathing — Y. P. No. 2
- Upper or clavicular breathing — Y. P. No. 3

By practising every morning and evening and by adding one count every week you will be able to easily reach a count of 8 or 10 seconds in each of the above mentioned pranayamas in about two months time. You are now in a position to combine all the three in Yogendra Pranayama No. 1 and involve all the respiratory muscles beginning with the diaphragm, intercostal and clavicular breaths, without any exaggerated movements. By doing this, the entire respiratory system and the three distinct parts of the lungs—superior, middle and inferior lobes—gets thoroughly ventilated as the chest cavity is expanded in all directions as shown by arrows in Fig 12.

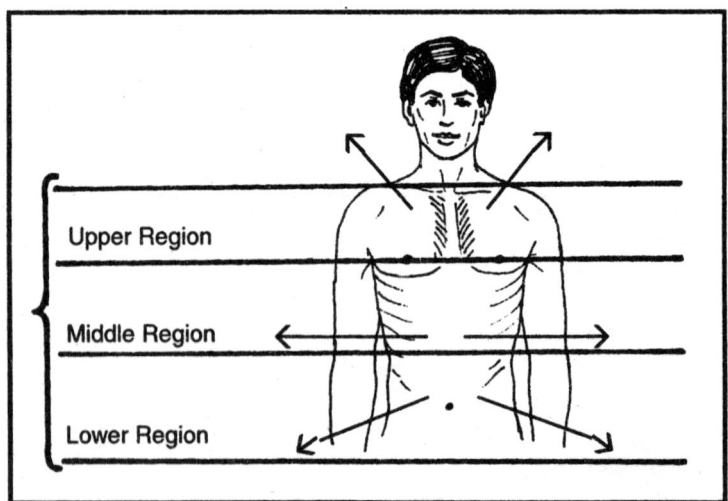

Fig 12 The Yogic Complete Breath from Three Levels or Regions

The most important is intercostal diaphragmatic breathing (Y.P. No. 4 + Y.P. No. 2) and add to this a little upper region breathing (clavicular breathing).

Method
- Sit in any meditative posture (Sukhasana/Vajrasana).

Breathing in
- First breath in from the lower region through diaphragmatic breathing, pushing the front wall of the abdomen a little, to a count of 5 (diaphragm pushed down).
- Then expand the lower part of the ribs (middle region) outwards and forwards by intercostal breathing to a count of 5 or to your comfortable capacity (the rib-cage is expanded).
- Finally, add another count of 5 through clavicular breathing (upper region) by raising slowly the collar bones, shoulders and lifting the bony cage vertically. This will fill the upper portion of the chest (apical portion of the lungs).

Breathing Out
- Holding the chest, exhale first by drawing the abdomen in, then relax the expanded portion of the lower ribs and finally the upper chest along with the shoulders, to normal position.

Frequency
Do it in the beginning for 5 rounds and gradually increase it to a maximum of 10 rounds. Equalise to a count of 15 seconds and maintain this rhythm. Count numbers mentally with each round.

Note: It is important to note that all this is one movement from lower to upper and not three different types of movements in instalments or with jerks—one moved in coordination with the second and the second with the third. There must be ease and a finer control of the respiratory movement, done without strain. Equalisation is a must to keep a steady rhythm.

18
Means of Relaxation

The modern complexities of life, with its stress and strain, have made living a constant source of conflict and tension. In a big city with its usual busy life accompanied by hurry and worry and a constant struggle for existence, the common man, many a time, feels tired and exhausted. Tension seems to cripple him and he finds himself unable to cope with his day-do-day work. It is common sense that body and mind, which are in constant activity, need some sort of relaxation, as a stop-gap process. But unfortunately this art of relaxation is not known to many. People are agitated, temperamental, sentimental and emotional. People who have greater responsibilities and ambitions lead a life which is even more active. It is this type of condition that causes more harm and leaves an evident impact on both the body and the mind.

Rest is the Principle of Relaxation

In any case, it is necessary that you should take a break and rest for a while to avoid exhaustion. The wear and tear of the body is compensated for by nature when you sleep. This helps in maintaining a steady rhythm of life. It is in this way that efficiency is maintained at the level of the body and the mind. But many people do not sleep till midnight, or their sleep is disturbed by dreams or external environmental factors. Sometimes it may be some worry that keeps them awake till late at night. They perhaps resort to sleeping pills which are used widely in the West. This is because natural sleep does not come to them. The chemicals contained in these sleeping pills (tranquillizers) are harmful for the brain and they can do damage to an extent that cannot be foretold. Remember, what is needed more than sleep is rest.

Quiet Entertainment makes for Real Relaxation

The recreating process aims to relax the body and the mind. This recreation can be more physical and less mental or vice versa. Football, for example, is a game; you may be enjoying it but you are using more energy. Similarly, playing chess seriously may involve much mental preoccupation. You must understand that leisurely quiet entertainment relaxes you where there is no spirit of competition or show. Swimming is a very recreative process. A walk through a park, a climb on a little hillock, a trip to the beach or anything wherein you seek a change of scene and activity are all well worth planning. The housewife in the middle of her neverending chores equally needs such short breaks. Spending time in gardening provides both physical and mental recreation. One must, however, avoid entertainment which leads to excitement and results in exhaustion.

The Basic Problem is one of Tension

Everything seems to be geared to tension. We work under tension, eat under tension, love under tension and we even rest under tension! Tension seems to be the root cause of ill health—physical and mental. The nerves cannot relax because of their fixed grip on the muscles and the muscles cannot relax because the nerves are tense. In purely physical tension, there is a constriction of muscles whether at work or at play; restriction in joint flexibility and in breathing; poor circulation, pain, irritability. This may result in hyperactivity of organs bringing about some physio-chemical changes in the physiological system. But in the present-day keyed-up existence, there is a constant nervous tension originating from the mind which is expressed through our nervous system. The mind having a vicious hold on the body does not allow muscular and bodily relaxation. It may be mental agitation and conflict, anxiety and worry or you may be pushed around due to lack of emotional stability.

Tension can be divided into two categories: neuro-muscular and mental, either of which becomes an oppressive barrier in the art of relaxation.

Tension is Disease: Relaxation is its Cure

"We call the relaxation practices psychosomatic practices. These practices will bring about a state of neuro-muscular relaxation with an increase in the energy content of the body, in the shortest possible time. They relieve us of psychosomatic disturbances and give us a feeling of freshness, provide energy, physical rest and mental poise. It quickly recuperates, regalvanises the nerve centres, collects the scattered forces, and reinvigorates the whole body."

— Shri Yogendraji

19
Psychosomatic Practices

Rest is the Principle of Relaxation
(Savasana : The Corpse Posture)

The first and second stages of general relaxation

Method
Lie down flat on your back with arms slightly away from your body (maybe 10 to 12 inches or more). The legs should be straight and relaxed. The heels should be kept apart, the feet turned slightly outwards, the ankles loose. The palms should be open and should face upwards. Relax all parts. Focus your attention to different parts of the body one after the other and feel if these are relaxed. Relax the legs, feet, arms, hands, palms; check that the shoulders are flat; head and neck carefully adjusted to a comfortable position. Lie still and concentrate on the sense of ease and comfort in those limbs, as they rest idly on the floor. Create a 'let go' sensation.

Once the body becomes comfortable, breathe deeply and evenly for some time and keep concentrating on the looseness and sense of repose in the limbs. Associate the feeling of sinking further and further into the ground with each exhalation and let go all resistance against the pull of gravity. Now remain still and quiet. Let the breathing be normal, slow and without any interference. Feel the tension and fatigue going out of the body with each exhalation. Continue for 10 minutes till the body becomes heavy or light.

Rhythm
Normal breathing.

Frequency
8 to 10 minutes.

Benefits
Provides complete rest and muscular relaxation. Transfers energy from overused parts to other vital organs; helps in psychosomatic disorders; induces better sleep.

Limitations
This is not recommended for persons with low blood pressure. Such persons and also those who feel uncomfortable in Savasana may revert to the practice of Nishpanda Bhava (a meditation practice) mentioned later on.

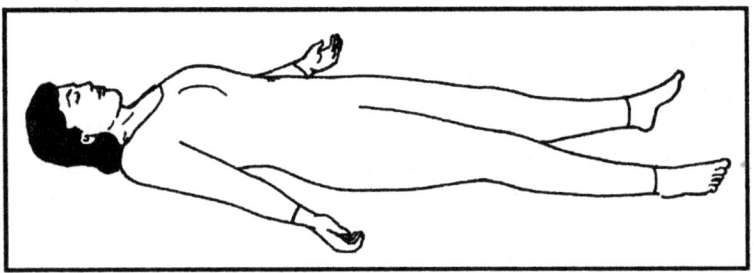

Fig 13

Third Stage of General Relaxation

Method
After doing the first two stages, working on the principle of 'let go', and relaxing particular parts, in this third stage conscious attention is withdrawn by stages from the sixteen vital zones of the body, from the toes to the top of the skull. At each zone stay for 30 seconds approximately—visualise the part, its shape, size, texture, colour, etc., and then withdraw the impulse and take it to the next part till you complete all the zones in this particular sequence. Repeat the cycle for any residual tension that may be left over. Attend to normal rhythmic breathing.

The zones are:

1. Toes
2. Ankles
3. Knees
4. Thighs (simultaneously with the arms)
5. Anus
6. Generative organ
7. Navel
8. Stomach
9. Heart
10. Neck
11. Lips
12. Tip of the nose
13. Eyes
14. Space between the eyebrows
15. Forehead
16. Top of the skull

Duration
8 to 10 minutes.

Benefits
Establishes muscular equilibrium and complete relaxation; renews strength and reinvigorates the whole body; good for building up heart tissues; pulse-rate and blood pressure go down; helps in psychosomatic disorders.

Makarasana (The Crocodile Posture)
(Recommended for women for partial relaxation)

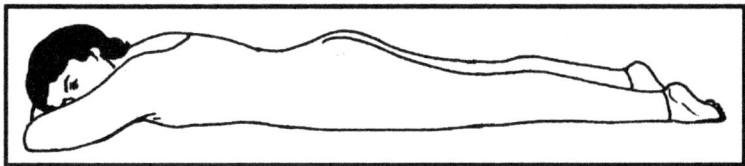

Fig 14

Method
Lie down flat on the ground, on your abdomen. Legs need to be stretched full length but partially separated. Arms should be folded and head should rest thereon. Work on the principle of 'let go' and offer no resistance against the pull of gravity. Direct your attention to the lower parts of your body—the toes, the calves, thighs, etc.,— and gradually move upwards to the head. Close the eyes and remain motionless. Put your mind to breathing and let the body consciousness fade away. Remain placid and motionless.

Rhythm
Breathing ought to be slow, normal and rhythmic.

Duration
10-15 minutes—practise it at midday or in the evening.

Benefits
Good posture for rest; good muscular relaxation; transfer of energy from overused parts to other vital organs; helps in psychosomatic disorders; induces better sleep.

Remember...
- Relaxation is always easier after exercise or when a little fatigue has set in.
- Choose a quiet spot where you will be free from interruptions.
- Mental strain is reduced when you are able to relax all the muscles of the body.
- Avoid numbness creeping in upon any part of the body due to prolonged immobility.
- Develop an attitude of 'let-go'. The underlying principle is to turn our will and life to the care of God and let a calm, peaceful feeling prevail—an oceanic feeling.
- The more we make relaxation a pleasure, as well as a duty, the better for us.
- Remember, how well one rests is more important than how long one sleeps.

Some Important Tips...
- If one works despite being tired, one uses three times the usual amount of energy—the damage is greater. Standing is more tiring than walking. Dodging a job gives you double fatigue.
- A heavy dinner at night is not advisable. Due to digestion problems, gases and gurgling, sleep is disturbed. Take food one hour before going to bed. No burden on memory should be carried before retiring, like reading an exciting novel or entertaining romantic ideas. The mind and the body should be kept free as far as possible from any pressure—social, economic, environmental, emotional, political, etc.

20
Food and Yoga

Mind is the Product of What one Eats

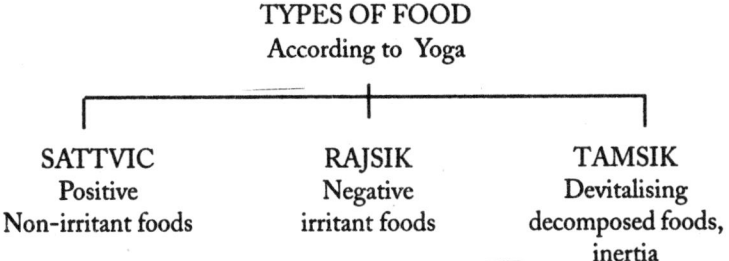

TYPES OF FOOD
According to Yoga

SATTVIC	RAJSIK	TAMSIK
Positive	Negative	Devitalising
Non-irritant foods	irritant foods	decomposed foods, inertia

Sattvic
Pure, agreeable, nourishing and easily digestible. It promotes purity of mind and inner strength and is conducive to higher thinking and pure intelligence. It keeps the body in harmony and mind calm and gives you a cool temperament.

Rajsik
Heavy protein and fats which are difficult to digest and assimilate. The body has to waste energy. It excites emotions; causes disease, grief and pain and binds the soul through attachment to actions and their fruits.

Tamsik
Stale and devitalising food. Processed and tinned foods. Also, consumption of reheated food leads to inertia and dullness and poisons the system. It binds the soul through error, sloth and sleep.

According to Pandit Shiv Sharma, "The sattvic diet aids in the formation of the mind, ie., the essence of the food is for the mind and the rest of it for the body."

Yoga has prescribed its own balanced diet of pure, light and nutritious food. Four principles to be borne in mind in the choice of food are: (1) Wholesomeness, (2) Freshness, (3) Alkalinity, and (4) Medicinal Value.

Remember, always eat qualitywise, not quantitywise.

Selection of Foodstuffs According to Yogic Diet

Food Groups	*Foodstuffs*
Cereals	Wheat is preferable to rice, jowar, bajra, etc. Prepare chapatis made of whole-wheat grain. It is a good source of carbohydrates.
Milk	Milk is a complete food and so it must not be avoided. Dairy products such as butter, buttermilk, curd, cheese, ghee—all are recommended. Milk is valued for its protein, vitamin and mineral contents. For the vegetarian, it is the only source of animal or first-class proteins.
Pulses	Moong (green/black) dal is easy to digest and is therefore preferable to chana, tur, masoor, etc. Beans also are a good source of protein, especially soyabean which has 43 per cent protein and a good amount of iron and Vitamin B Complex. Sprouted pulses are good sources of Vitamin C.

Vegetables

Five most beneficial vegetables which are excellent sources of vitamins and minerals are:

Spinach	Provides iron, vitamins, calcium and protein-building amino-acids. Other leafy vegetables like chowlai, methi (fenugreek), and salad greens and raddish (mooli) also contain minerals and vitamins.

Lady's Finger (Bhindi)	Useful in all irritable states of intestines and for the genito-urinary organs.
Wildsnake-gourd (Parwal)	For vitality and vigour.
Brinjal (Baigan)	Remedy for liver complaints.
Bitter-gourd (Karela)	Excellent blood purifier. Good for gout, rheumatism and diseases of the spleen and liver. Medical doses of karela juice are recommended as a remedy for diabetes.
Roots and Tubers	Potatoes with jacket, suran (yam elephant), beetroot and carrots are sources of carbohydrates. Carrots contain Vitamin A, while potatoes have iron, magnesium, Vitamin B and C.
Sugar and Jaggery	Jaggery (gur) and honey are preferable to white sugar.* These are a good source of carbohydrates and concentrated sources of energy.
Fruits	Citrus and other fruits are recommended except jackfruit which has fibres and is difficult to digest. Avoid acidic, sour or unripe fruits. Fruits are a good source of vitamins.
Dry Fruits	Dates, figs, raisins, almonds, apricots, etc., are good sources of vitamins, if not treated chemically. They are also rich in carbohydrates and minerals.
Oils and Fats	It is better to use mustard, gingelly or sunflower oil for cooking. These contain fat.
Spices and Condiments	As far as possible spices and condiments, etc., should be avoided as these have been found to have a stimulating effect and act as irritants and are harmful. Similarly, highly seasoned stuffs, exciting and intoxicating drinks are prohibited.

---

* White Sugar — Dr Henry Schroeder, an eminent biochemist, is of the opinion that refining of raw sugar into white sugar removes 93 per cent of the ash which leads to chromium deficiency—one of the causes of the hardening of arteries and consequent heart disease.

Tea and Coffee — Tea and coffee and acidic. The practice of taking them immediately after major meals is bad. Caffeine in coffee and tea has a stimulating effect. As far as possible, one should restrict it to only two cups a day.

The ideal food for man is the food which contributes to greater endurance, is revitalising and health-promoting. It consists of grains, dairy products like milk, curd (yoghurt), buttermilk and cottage cheese, vegetables, carrot and beetroot and lots of salad, fresh fruits, nuts, honey and nutritive roots.

How to Get the Best out of Food

- *Green and Yellow Vegetables*
  These are mostly full of Vitamin A. Spinach contains a lot of iron which we need for the haemoglobin in red blood corpuscles (RBCs). It can be better absorbed if it is taken together with Vitamin C. For instance, a dash of lemon on palak-ki-bhaji.
- *Raw Vegetables (Salads)*
  Use raw vegetables made of chopped carrots, onions, raddish (mooli), cucumber, a little tomato and chutneys in which mint (pudina) is used.
- *Vital Group of 'B' Vitamins*
  Hand-pounded rice, unpolished wheat, dals (pulses) and green leafy vegetables.
- *Fermentation*
  Fermentation is used everywhere in India in making curd, batter for dosa, idli, etc. Fermentation multiplies the contents of vitamins several fold, increases iron availability and greatly improves the digestibility of the starch and proteins in food.
- *Vitamin C*
  Good and cheap sources of this vitamin are amla (gooseberry), lemon juice and raw onions. Guava contains six times as much Vitamin C as six oranges, but one amla contains twice as much as guava. Remember Vitamin C is destroyed by cooking and exposure to sunlight.
  Sprouting or germination is a simple way of increasing the Vitamin C content and digestibility of many foodstuffs. Green

gram Phaseolus Radiatus (moong) germinated is very rich in Vitamin C.

To sprout seeds at home, add water (one-half to an equal quantity) to the moong or Bengal gram and leave for 8 to 16 hours till fully absorbed. Tie the swollen grains in a muslin cloth, place on a plate and invert a wire bowl over it and allow it to sprout for 12 to 24 hours.

- *Protein*
Soyabean flour contains 40 per cent protein; peas, lentils and dried beans between 20 and 25 per cent. Use a little curd or buttermilk with each meal to boost protein quantity.
- *Vitamin D*
It is found in cheese, curds and milk and all varieties of greens. It is formed on the skin when exposed to sunlight, which is needed for strong bones and calm nerves. Strip and sunbathe your naked body for at least 15 minutes every morning or evening or wear white clothes, preferably khadi, when exposed to sunlight.
- Replace tea or coffee with a decoction of tulsi leaves and ginger.

Quantity of Food

Moderation in diet (*mitahara*) is emphasised as the guideline. Eat no more or no less than what is absolutely necessary to satisfy one's appetite. Moreover, the yogis believe in filling only half the stomach with food, a quarter with water and leaving the rest for fermentative gases or air.

When to Eat

Food should be taken only when hungry. A light breakfast and two principal meals (lunch and dinner) are considered sufficient for a person leading a sedentary life. Between the intervals of the principal meals, it is advisable not to eat anything. Each time there should be a four-hour gap between breakfast, lunch, evening tea and dinner. It is advisable that no water be taken with food; it checks digestion and produces indigestion. The best thing is to take water half an hour before or after a meal.

How to Eat

Masticate your food properly and learn to appreciate the natural taste and flavour of fruits and vegetables. It will also lessen the chances of overeating.

Remember, according to Shri Yogendraji, "impaired digestion results from taking foods wrongly selected in kind or in quantity, wrongly prepared or wrongly masticated."

Some Important Guidelines

Take

- Low-salt diet or less of salt.
- Low-fat dairy products and especially yoghurt and buttermilk.
- A generous helping of leafy and green vegetables and fresh fruits everyday.
- Sprouted seeds should be included in the menu at least twice a week. These are rich in Vitamins C, A, E, K and several of the B Complex group.
- Take half a teaspoon of honey in your tea. It is rapidly and easily assimilated and is a heart and muscle stimulant.

Avoid

- Processed, refined sugar and synthetic foodstuffs.
- Eating snacks and other tidbits between meals.
- Fat, rich meat, pork, egg yolk, prawns and shellfish.
- White bread, strong tea, coffee, all types of condiments, tinned foods, biscuits and cakes, puddings, processed cheese, fried foods, soft drinks.
- Avoid use of baking soda as it destroys vitamins.
- Avoid drinking water while eating (or during meals).
- Avoid deep-fried foods like pakoras, puris, and samosas.
- Avoid aluminium utensils for cooking.

Do Not

- Eat when your are not hungry.
- Eat when angry or emotionally upset.
- Eat when you are to do work immediately after a meal.
- Eat foods containing colouring or flavouring agents.

Do

- Try to relax a little, after the day's work, before commencing your meal.
- Take plenty of time over your meal and masticate your food thoroughly.

Remember...

- Missing an evening meal once a week is beneficial.
- The risk factors in the development of coronary heart disease, strokes, kidney disease and diabetes are:
  — Overweight
  — High cholesterol levels
  — Cigarette smoking
  — Lack of exercise
  — Hypertension
- Overeating and overweight go hand in hand with lack of exercise.
- One ounce of body fat equals about 219 calories. If you want to reduce, cut your calorie intake by 500 calories a day. You should lose about 1 pound a week or 4 pounds in a month. It is safe.
- Slimming foods can cause both physical and pyschological damage.
- Vegetables should be baked, steamed or prepared in a pressure cooker. Food should not be overcooked.
- Food material should not be extremely hot, cold or excessively spiced.
- In any kind of abuse, be it in food, alcohol or tobacco, the body is the sufferer.

Part IV
Your Stress Factor

21
Psychosomatic Problems

'Psyche' and 'soma' are Greek words meaning the mind and the body respectively. So psychosomatic diseases are those diseases which, while they have their origin in the psyche, are clinically diagnosed through somatic symptoms manifested in the body. In simple words, they are 'mind-body' problems which have simultaneous interaction and mutual influence. Generally, it is believed that it is the emotional effects, caused by the stress and tension of modern life which are translated into somatic disorders. Ulcers, nerve and heart disorders, migraines, headaches, asthma, colitis, eczema, diabetes, disorders of the digestive system, etc., are among the common psychosomatic complaints.

Stress Diseases Expressed in Psychophysiological Reactions

Psychosomatic diseases are now called Stress Diseases expressed through psychophysiological reactions and are very much linked with personality patterns, for example, in the Ulcer Personality there are psychophysiologic gastrointestinal reactions to life-situations. It is said that a feeling of strong resentment, sustained hostility and anxiety (by parasympathetic overcompensation) results in a perceptible increase of acid production (HCL) which eats away the stomach lining or the lining of the duodenum, leaving a kind of wound. The anxiety is often intensified by a sense of responsibility associated with being in authority as in the case of ambitious individuals like business executives or successful tycoons. In the

Asthmatic Personality, there is a psychophysiologic respiratory reaction to certain oppressing life-situations. The airways become congested and breathing becomes difficult. Hypersensitive, insecure individuals, afraid of losing love and protection or having difficulties in obtaining the needed love and support, are generally victims of this anxiety-borne disease.

22

Emotional States Affect the Body's Defences

To understand the problem more clearly we can say there is an interplay of three factors, as shown in the following diagram:

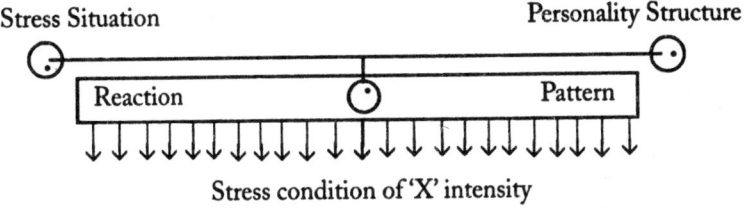

Stress condition of 'X' intensity
Expressed in terms of worry, anxiety, depression, fear, etc.

Your individual personality complex, on meeting any oppressing stress situation, creates within you a reaction pattern in terms of worry, anxiety, fear, depression, etc., resulting in a Stress Condition of 'X' intensity. Why 'X' intensity? Because it is going to differ from person to person. Even situations which cause tension to one individual may not cause any tension to another person. Stress produces its effect upon the body through the pituitary and the adrenal glands as they equip the body to the tremendous task of flight or fight. Excessive stimulation of the endocrine glands and the nervous system results in impairment of physiological functioning expressed in terms of malfunctioning of some part or organ whichever happens to be the weakest in the individual organism. It is the weaker link which always gives way. Aided by

new biochemical techniques and a vastly-expanded understanding of immunology and neurochemistry, the fast growing field of research and studies shows that emotions acting through the brain can affect:
- The nervous system
- The hormone levels
- The immunological responses

This changes the individual's susceptibility to a host of organic illnesses. A strong mind-body linkage has been proved once and for all and that has put to rest the Cartesian dichotomy that had separated body and mind since the 17th century. Dr George F. Solomon, a psychiatrist at the University of California has said, "Mind and body are inseparable. The brain influences all sorts of physiological processes that were once thought as not being centrally regulated." With the increasing concern over the "Stress Epidemic" in the USA, numerous new fields have sprung up: behavioural medicine to battle stress-related illnesses, psychoneuroimmunology to explore the way emotional states affect the body's defences, etc. Furthermore, a person under stress takes a longer time to heal from a given disease than a person who is not under stress. The process of ageing is also accelerated under conditions of stress.

In any case, prolonged stress (mental or emotional) in any form plays an important part in the development and final outcome of almost any disease of the body, be it the common cold or cancer. Stress generally comes into play either during loss or when there is threat to individual status, goals, health, job, security, etc. There are different forms of stresses in day-to-day life. Some of the stress-producting events are:
- *Death*
   Death of one's spouse or of a close relative, marital separation, divorce, marriage, etc.
- *Home*
   Trouble with in-laws; family conflict and tension; illness, sickness, etc., in family; even change in living condition, etc.

- *Office*
  Trouble with boss, inability to handle subordinates, losing job, business readjustment, change in financial status, etc.

So there are different forms of stresses in day-to-day life. Under conditions of worry and anxiety, overwork, fatigue and chronic infections, some people, even if they pull on for sometime, break down inflicted by different diseases, either singly or in combination. Some develop high blood pressure, others hardening of the blood vessels and coronary heart disease, and yet others rheumatoid arthritis, etc.

23
Internally Generated Pressure

Yoga was the first system in the world to recognise the connection and the interaction between the body and the mind. It tells you that the mind influences the body much more than the body influences the mind, a fact which is clearly witnessed in psychosomatic and psychiatric disorders. An important thing to remember is that stress is measured and evaluated in terms of how it is experienced by the person himself or, in other words, what the event means to that person. It is when a person fails to adjust to his emotional or psychological conflicts, and the stress is prolonged and far exceeds the level of tolerance, that a person develops what can be called as *critical stress*, and if he cannot cope with it, then either the mind or the body has to break down and that is when the following happens:

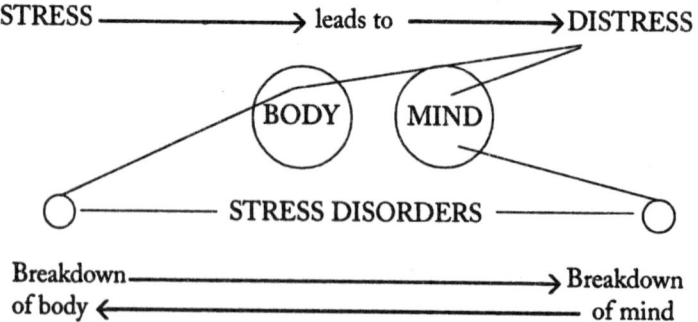

An interesting feature of the 1971 medical study report prepared by the research unit of the Yoga Institute, Santa Cruz, Bombay, was that most of the patients suffered not much from external stress. The problems mainly had arisen from internal stresses caused by conflicts and complexes in relation to the self. It is all an internally generated pressure. One has to understand the sources of stress and tension within an individual. The causes of restlessness and tension are often deeply embedded in our lifestyle and our personality complex, our thinking, feeling, temperament, disposition, basic values and attitudes. Most of the 'pressure' comes from within ourselves. Situations which cause tension to one individual may not cause tension to others. It seems it is not the situation but we ourselves, who have to take the blame. We seem to be aware of tension only at the level of its symptoms rather than its causes. The symptoms appear at the site of the organ but the cause generally lies elsewhere in the subtle body and in the yogic sense, this cause lies in the Chitta—the Personality Complex. What is significant in a stress condition is that "the degree of mental and emotional stress produced in an individual going through a stress-producing situation depends to a large extent on how he or she is habituated to react to it. "This is important irrespective of the situation and the profession." Yoga tries to re-educate the patient to alter his habitual reaction pattern, develop a coping mechanism and thus holds the key to better living. Yoga has laid down psychosomatic means through various psychophysiological processes for dealing with the body-mind complex. It tries to harmonise and integrate the human personality at all levels and stages of life.

Conclusion: 'Man is What his Mind is'

"The problem of man is man himself; everything done for him outside of himself is of no real help to him", says Shri Yogendraji.

The mind is a bundle of *samskaras* (root potentials, tendencies) ideas, habits, impulses and emotions. According to yoga, once the mind becomes calm and steady, clarity improves and a person becomes more aware of the forces which bring about disturbances. He is thus mentally better equipped to deal with any situation; with a tranquil mind he remains unperturbed in difficult moments, even when the external factors remain unchanged.

Part V
A Technique for Achieving
Inner Tranquillity (Meditation)
(A serene, calm, tension-free state of mind)

24
Tranquillity Provides a Backdrop

Vritti Nirodha (Restraint of mental modifications) is the keynote of Yoga. To achieve this, the emphasis is laid on two important aspects of mind—Purity and Tranquillity. Because the mind is a bundle of samskaras, ideas, habits, impulses and emotions, the state of tranquillity according to Shri Yogendraji provides a backdrop. The ethical purity (*Chitta-shuddhi*) through *Yamaniyama* is a preliminary step and will help the individual to get rid of ignoble traits of his character. One has to develop pure and sincere love in the heart without any selfish desires. Another basic element in our yoga *sadhana* is to cultivate a habit of stilling the mind. Our pranayama, special psychosomatic and meditation practices, will help you as a quietening process and will habituate the mind, if we persevere in keeping the mind calm most of the time. Besides, these will promote steadiness, which is the central feature of all yoga practices. We are sure achieve a state of tranquillity.

"In fact, this state of tranquillity, which is itself a transformation of the earlier states of disjointed mental activities, provides a backdrop, against which we can evaluate our earlier and later thought processes, better," says Dr Jayadevji Yogendra. The state of tranquillity is expressed beautifully in these words:

With her dwelleth peace, with her dwelleth safety and contentment; she is cheerful, but not gay; serious but not grave; she vieweth the joys and the sorrows of life with an equal and steady eye.

— Anonymous

Let us proceed step by step to achieve this state of tranquillity and steadiness of the mind. The first step is to give rest to your turbulent mind through the practice of *Pratyahara* or withdrawal of the senses. The senses distract the forces in the system within and retard focussing of consciousness. Pratyahara (mental abstraction) is the fifth step of the eightfold path of Yoga. Let us suppose that one is driving a chariot drawn by five wild horses and that each horse is trying to pull the chariot it its own direction. Is it possible for one to keep the chariot on a steady course? The answer is 'yes' provided one has the reins of all the five horses, firmly in one's hands, and, provided one has enough knowledge and practice in controlling horses.

In the Katha Upanishad, the body is described as the chariot, the mind as the reins, the intellect as the charioteer, the senses as the horses, and the objects of the senses as their road. The self is the rider, seated on the chariot. Unless the rider has understanding and can make the charioteer control his horses, he can never attain his goal, but the senses, like vicious steeds, will drag him where they please and may even destroy him.

— Swamy Vivekananda
(*The Complete Works of Swami Vivekananda*, Vol. 8, page 43)

Yoni Mudra (Symbol of the Embryo)

This is a special psychosomatic practice, to control the sense. It functions as a symbolic seal to shut off the sense organs.

Method

Sit it the meditative posture of *Sukhasana*. Raise your hands to your face, keeping your elbows in line with your shoulders. To withdraw the senses, lightly press the ear openings (lobes) with your thumbs; keeping the index fingers on the eyelashes after closing the eyes. There should be no undue strain. Press the bridge of the nose with the middle fingers; the area just above the upper lip with the ring fingers and the area just below the lower lip with the little fingers. Remain in this position motionless for as long as possible. Listen to your breathing sound or any other sound vibrating in the ears or within the body.

Fig 15

Rhythm
Normal breathing.

Duration
10 to 15 minutes.

Benefits
Gives rest to a turbulent mind, conserves energy, controls external senses, induces joy of solitude, leads to pratyahara (abstraction); develops an attitude of fortitude or *tapa*.

Limitations
Don't do this asana if you are suffering from cervical spondylitis or from acute depression.

Remember...
- Don't put pressure on the eyes or on the eyeballs.
- Regulate breathing by exercising a light pressure on either side of the nose.
- In case you feel uncomfortable at your lower back or find it difficult to keep the spine straight, take the support of a wall.
- You may drop your elbows and hands when you feel too tired or too much pain in the shoulders, but don't open your eyes.
- Having rested for 30 seconds, resume again. Remember, it is also a practice of endurance.
- 10 minutes of Yoni Mudra is to be followed by 5 minutes of Sukhasana or Savasana.

25
Meditation

The keynote of meditation is *chittavrittinirodha*—elimination of the *vrittis* or modulations that keep surging in *chit* in the forms of ripples.

Each individual is a bundle of sensations, thoughts and ideas which are always in a state of flux. *Chitta,* which is a subtle substance of matter, always exists in the form of its states which are called *vrittis*. It undergoes modifications and this has to be stopped and controlled and then alone will the *chitta* be able to come in contact with pure consciousness. Abiding in this state will give you lasting peace and supreme happiness by destroying all afflictions (*Kleshas*). It can further lead you on to perfection and the highest knowledge of discrimination (*Prajna*) which will dispel all ignorance. To achieve this goal one has to prepare oneself and finally create a *sattvic* condition of mind for spiritual unfoldment and to achieve a higher state of consciousness. We relate below some of the objectives with the various practices learnt so far.

- The usefulness of a code of subjective ethics through *Yamaniyama* to purify the ordinary mind.
- The practice of inwardness through the meditative posture for emotional shut-off.
- Psychophysical control of the human organisers and maintenance of its steadiness and strength through meaningful participation in a postural training programme (*asanas*) and pranayamas.

- Lastly, the control of senses through the special psychosomatic practice of Yoni Mudra. All these elements cumulatively help us to reduce physical, mental and emotional tensions. One has to achieve a balanced steady mind—a state that makes for strength and power and deep understanding. Remember, unsteadiness of mind encourages the disease process.

Now we wish to create a deep sense of tranquillity through the various practices of meditation to give you a variety of worthwhile experiences besides cleaning the mind of all it habitual thought-waves, unrest and emotions. During psychosomatic and meditative practices it has been noticed that there is a drop in heart activity and rate of breathing. Favourable changes occur in the brain pattern as well. All such practices are good for coping with physical and mental illnesses, like neuroses, psychoses, nervous breakdowns and high blood pressure and other psychosomatic disorders.

Yogendra Nishpanda Bhava (Motionless State of Mind)
(From sound to inner calmness, passivity and stillness of mind)

By learning to condition the mind through meditative postures described in the beginning of the course, you may have achieved some progress. The amount of thoughts and their intensity must have considerably reduced, if you have practised for a sufficiently long period. This reduces nervous agitation and quietens the mind.

However, in Yogendra Nishpanda Bhava you have to make use of the sense of hearing (mechanics of sound) and, through it, achieve still greater quietness of mind—a condition which no disturbance can affect. Sit in a relaxed position, reclining against a wall, listen to a sound of low intensity, a rhythmic sound or a sound of the fading-out kind (like the sound of a passing car or aeroplane). This listening is to be done in a passive manner. This passivity, when it deepens, leads to a deeper quietness where the hold of the mind on the body is loosened and it withdraws, narrowing the beam of consciousness.

Nis   :   Negative
Panda :   Movement
Bhava :   State of Mind

Method
Sit relaxed reclining against the wall. Adjust your legs, feet, arms and hands to a comfortable position. Sit motionless and feel quiet. Focus on a sound—preferably a low-intensity one or a fading sound or a rhythmic sound, for example, the sound made by a timepiece. Cultivate the passive attitude of listening. Remain passive and get completely absorbed in the sound.

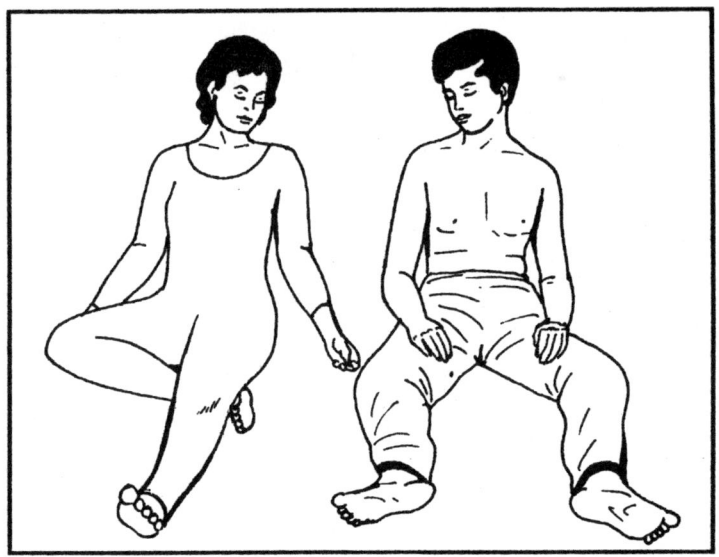

Fig 16

Rhythm
Normal breathing.

Duration
10 to 15 minutes.

Benefits
Introspective training of the mind; release of tension; feeling of being physically and mentally relaxed; subjective experience of quietude; ideal technique for cultivating passivity.

Note: One can do it sitting on a chair or a sofa in the office or at home.

Remember...
- It is important to assume a very comfortable position so that you are able to retain the posture for a considerable length of time without any need to change it.
- One can follow a real or imaginary sound. The sound selected should be constant, rhythmic and feeble like the chirping of birds, or the ticking of a wall clock, dripping water, or a fan.

Fig 17

- Office goers and housewives can do it after lunch. Those who don't have sound sleep or have disturbed sleep or are suffering from sleeplessness should do it at night before going to bed.
- When you are listening to the sound, refuse to do anything else, keep yourself quiet and let your mind get absorbed in the sound.
- Remember what Sri Aurobindo had said, "calm peaceful silence is more productive than meditation."

26
Meditate to Open Yourself to the Divine Power

Japa Yoga (Mantra)
This is based on the technique of sound.
A *japa* is a natural mantra and is easiest to practise on the mantra '*Soham*': (That I am). This mantra has to be synchronised with your breathing.

Concept
This is to invoke the thought power through the subtle vibrations of sound for unification of the individual with the divine Universal Power.

Method
Sit in the meditative posture of Sukhasana. Close your eyes adopting a passive attitude. Simply watch your breathing for some time. Now repeat this mantra Soham synchronising it with your breathing. Breathe in with *So* and breathe out with *Ham;* the breathing should be even and natural.

Duration
5 to 10 minutes.

Contemplation
Contemplate on the spiritual significance of the mantra and pay attention to each breath, as it naturally goes on. Imagine that while breathing out, the individual self goes out with the sound of *Ham* in order to be identified with or merged in the *Vishwatma* or

Parmatma and while breathing in with *So* comes back into the consciousness of individuality, bringing, as it were, the Universal Spirit into itself.

Benefits
With the practice of this *Ajapa Japa* Yogi Gorakhanath says, "all lust, hatred, malice, fear, anxiety and restlessness vanish, and the bliss of the consciousness of self-fulfilment is enjoyed within the heart".

Note: In case the mind is very restless then first do Yoni Mudra for 5 to 10 minutes followed by a minimum of 5 minutes of the Ajapa Japa. Do it in the morning or in the evenings.

Aum (Sound Symbol)
Meditate to establish a link with the supreme spirit through *Pranava-Japa*: *Aum* is the first sound—the unproduced and undifferentiated natural eternal sound of the universe. It is the most spontaneous self-expression of energy or power in audible form. It is the source and the basis of all syllabi, words and sentences. It is taught in the *Katho Upanishad* that Aum phonetically is a blended expression of three sounds: (A) (OO) and (M). Its japa represents the creative principle of unfailing and infinite potency for the achievement of success, prosperity and well-being of mankind.

Rishi Dayananda explains the meaning of *Aum* as follows:
(A)   symbolises Virat, Agni, Universes, etc.
(OO)   symbolises Hiranya Garbha, Ether, Air, etc.
(M)   symbolises Creator, Sun, Consciousness, Intelligence, etc.

Method
Listen to Aum and meditate deeply upon it. With the eyes closed sit in a meditative posture. The first letter 'A' is uttered from the back of the mouth. The second letter 'U' is uttered from the middle of the mouth. The last word 'M' is uttered by closing the lips. You chant the word *Aum* in a single blended expression with a steady and lengthened utterance such as AAA... UUU... MMM... and continue even after M till the sound fades out with a humming sound. Fill up the whole atmosphere with the sweet and melodious

sound of Aum. While breathing in, synchronise the breath by mentally pronouncing Aum and again chant Aum. Repeat it several times.

Duration
5 to 10 minutes, preferably early in the morning.

Benefits.
It improves breathing, especially the exhalation. Good for throat, tongue and nose. It improves the quality of your voice. R.L. Jamdagneya in his book *Swar Therapy* says: "The chanting of the word *Aum* generates Alpha, Beta and Gamma rays which have got healing properties. It activates and energises the various centres of the central nervous system."

Note: Never produce the sound from the throat and strain yourself. The sound should come from the middle of the chest making full use of your diaphragm.

The Japa of Gayatri Mantra

Another method to establish a link with the Supreme Spirit is through *Gayatri Japa*.

The Gayatri Mantra is the most unique, both in respect of its origin, popularity, value and effectiveness. It is the worship of the Supreme Creator and Lord, and it also contains a prayer for the divine purification and enrichment of the *buddhi* (intellect).

"By means of this mantra, man can secure the highest knowledge and power, directly from God—The Almighty Supreme", says Chiranjiv Lal in *The Grandeur of Gayatri*.

ॐ भूर्भुवः स्वः तत्सवितुर्वरेण्यं
भर्गो देवस्य धीमहि धियो योनः प्रचोदयात्।

Aum! bhoo-r-bhuvaḥ swaḥ tat-savitu-r-varényam bhargo dévasya dheemahi, dhiyo yo naḥ prachodayat.

"Aum. Let us meditate on the Glorious Effulgence of the Divine Being who has created this universe—May He enlighten our heart and direct our understanding."

Repeat this mantra aloud in solitude with devotion for five minutes and then mentally repeat it for 10 to 15 minutes at least by concentrating your thought upon its meaning.

Remember what Swami Sivananda had said, "Mantra-Japam is a powerful sadhana for controlling the mind and awakening the inner cosmic fire and psychic consciousness".

Remember...
- If you find it difficult to meditate with the eyes closed, focus on some object—a picture or sculpture, idol, or any other form which can arrest the mind.
- Say your chosen mantra aloud at first and repeat it over and over again; it will help you to concentrate. Then repeat the mantra silently.
- Before you start to do mantra japa, breathe slowly and rhythmically or do Yogendra Pranayama No. 1 for 10 rounds.

Part VI
Thought Control
and
Emotional Therapeutics

27
Thoughts are Forces

Your life is what your thoughts make of it.

— Marcus Aurelius

Our perverted thinking, negative thoughts and feelings, our wrong identification with the ego, and our unhealthy attitude play a major part in our mental make-up. Very often we act compulsively under strong emotions or fixed ideas. All these factors, according to Shri Yogendraji, "give rise to symptoms of anarchy, imperfection, disquietude and circumscription by which the higher planes of consciousness are continually shadowed." By controlling our mind and cultivating a positive attitude to govern our life, we can become captains of our ships, and can make it sail towards the harbour of Beauty, Harmony, Happiness and Success.

Thoughts are Forces

Discordant thoughts of ill health, vivid pictures of unfortunate physical conditions held in the mind, horrible thoughts of fear; the things we dread and are anxious about; the passions of anger, hatred, jealousy, envy, and greed, affect the integrity and functioning of the human organism. Many negative states of mind arise from a subconscious desire to escape from unfavourable circumstances. A great many people think they would be happy if they were only in different circumstances, when the fact is that circumstances have little, if anything, to do with one's temperament or disposition. What a man does in spite of circumstances, rather than because of them, is the measure of his ability. Also, we must have noticed how we get influenced by a person who is in a state of utter depression as a result of his negative thoughts and vibrations. Our thinking is also influenced by the conditions of life, in which we are placed, our socio-cultural environment, the tremendous advances of scientific discoveries, and the brainwashing and propaganda that goes on in the world of publicity and advertisement.

Thoughts are forces and the law that applies in this regard is that likes attract each other. Ralph Waldo Trine says, "We are continually attracting towards us from both the seen and the unseen side of life forces and conditions most akin to those of our own thoughts." Thought produces phenomena similar to those of electricity. Particles of living matter change from positive to negative by the influence of thought. Thought forces can change the mental and emotional conditions present in us and in the atmosphere surrounding us. This proves that if there is mind-made disease, there is also mind-made health. We all have to realise the power of the mind and the spirit. In mind-made health, the idea is to heal the mind, which in turn heals the body and becomes your own physician. The important question is: How do you live in your world of thoughts?

We must therefore think and learn to turn our thoughts to good use—change negative thoughts into positive ones, keeping the mind filled with bright, hopeful, loving, uplifting thoughts and express them in deeds.

28
Emotional Control

Emotional Therapeutics

There is a wide spectrum of Emotional Reaction Patterns ranging from Revolt to Depression—the two extremes as expressed by Sri Aurobindo. He says, "Any desire not satisfied, any impulse that knocks against an obstacle, any unpleasant contact with outside, creates very easily and very spontaneously a revolt or a depression, because it is the normal state of things—normal in present life."

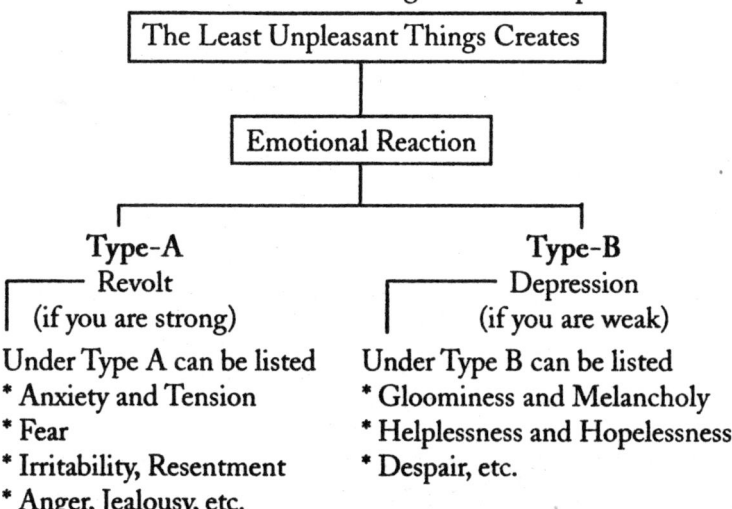

All these emotional reactions emanate from the mind due to mental afflictions (kleshas). Therefore their treatment also should be from the standpoint of the mind alone.

Such treatment is both sane and simple. We need to merely recognise that like produces like; that opposite emotions cannot exist in the mind at one and the same time and also that a positive thought and a positive attitude will drive out a negative one. In this great truth lies our health and happiness and it will also help banish fear and worry forever.

29
Our Destructive Emotions

Anger
If a person is overcome by anger, it creates a sort of a body thunderstorm which has a corresponding effect on the normal healthy and life-giving secretions of the body. These become poisonous and destructive. Anger in the mother may poison a nursing child.

The greatest antagonists that we come across in the path of self-realisation are *Kama* (desire) and *Krodha* (anger). Kama leads to Krodha. The egoistic 'I' asserts itself as 'I' and 'mine' in the mind, resulting in a false identification and gets caught up in the ever expanding desire complex (Kama) of highly personal ambitions to gain name, fame, status, wealth and coveting pleasures and passions. 'I' tries to gratify desire as and when it arises even at the expense of others, even eliminating whatever gets in its way. When any desire is thwarted 'I' naturally becomes blind with anger.

According to the *Gita* when a person is overpowered by wrath, he loses his mental equilibrium, as a direct consequence of *Moha*. From anger arises delusion or mental derangement (*Smriti Bhrama*). This leads to loss of reason, and from loss of reason he goes on to complete ruin. (*Bhagvad Gita*, Ch. 2/62-63).

Vipaksha Bhavana (Thinking of the ill-effects of anger)
Think it over before you give way to a fit of temper—just stop and think what a scene you are going to present before your friends or associates. You are going to present yourself as an absolute lunatic

for the time being. Does it pay? Does it pay to make such a fool of yourself, to make such an exhibition of the beast in you? Your uncontrolled temper may stand between you and your hopes, between you and success. Just notice how you tremble all over after a great fit of temper! And what it has cost you mentally... and so on.

> **Remember...**
> Anger hurts the one who is possessed by it more than the one against whom it is directed. The fire one kindles for one's enemy often burns oneself, rather than one's enemy.
> — Swamy Rajeshwarananda

Jealousy and Hatred

Feelings of hatred, revenge and animosity towards someone may at times be expressed in the stiffness of your joints and your rheumatic troubles.

"In the healing process of an ulcer, what the patient eats is probably far less important than what is eating him up."

To overcome jealousy and hatred: Try to be less selfish, possessive, impatient and self-centred. Practise the virtue of giving, sharing, caring and loving others.

Worry and Fear

Fear, says Dr William H. Holcomb, "has many degrees of gradation, from the state of extreme alarm, fright or terror, down to the slightest shade of apprehension of impending evil. But all along the line it is the same thing—a paralysing impression upon the centres of life which can produce, through the agency of the nervous system, a vast variety of morbid symptoms in every tissue of the body." Fear and worry are among the principal causes of stomach troubles.

Contemplation (Bhavana)

Think it over. Does worry pay? Have you ever gained anything by it? Aren't you tired of losing this precious, invaluable nerve energy which means so much in your vocation and which you also need in your life.

Think it Over (about fear): Try to understand what is it that you fear. It is always something that has not yet happened—something that is non-existent. In overcoming your fears, follow each one out to its logical conclusions. For example, fear of death, yes, death is a fact; we are born, we grow old and die. Don't dwell upon decay; like other fears—fear of accidents, of sickness, of poverty, of some terrible misfortune—and be haunted by the dread of some vague impending evil. Convince yourself that at the present moment the thing that you fear does not exist save in your imagination. Whether it will ever come to pass in the future or not, your fear is a waste of time, energy, bodily and mental strength. The natural antidote is *Courage* and *Confidence;* holding the opposite thought in the mind drives out the fear or neutralises it.

Depression

Thoughts of sickness and discordant moods contribute to disease. Sorrow retards blood circulation, respiration becomes slower, digestion is inspired and affects the bodily secretions and excretions. When your thought patterns are negative and distorted, you sink into acute unhappiness and discouragement, feeling miserable. You tend to discount everything, life loses interest and meaning and you may even have suicidal impulses.

The Need for Auto-conditioning

The first step is not to brood over your troubles; do not acknowledge in your thought that you are a failure, that you can't do anything worthwhile, that luck is against you... instead resolve not to go any further in that direction. The second step is to create a passive, receptive mind through the yogic techniques of deep relaxation, quietude and calmness. Then talk to your inner mind (subconscious mind) holding a hopeful, optimistic thought and a positive attitude, according to your particular problem, that you want to overcome. Use appropriate words to suit your special need. Tell yourself that you will grapple with your problem like a courageous man and will gather all the strength to come out of your 'blues' forever and feel cheerful. Let go of everything that is unpleasant, and has made you suffer. Resolve that no matter what happens you are going to be happy, that you are going to enjoy yourself. Whenever you think of yourself, always hold the image of yourself as you would like to be—have this kind of good heart-to-heart talks with yourself.

> ***Remember...***
> To neutralise and overcome these emotional stresses, you have to:
> - Learn the ability to relax at will through psychosomatic practices and meditation.
> - Change your thoughts; whenever a negative thought comes, promptly voice a positive one to cancel it out.
> - Acquire emotional control through contemplation and cultivate positive thoughts in order to weaken the potency of negative thoughts.
> - Bring about a fundamental change in your mental attitude.

Part VII
Guidelines for Living a Fuller Life

30
How to Carry on Your Work
(Your Action Potential)

Activity is synonymous with life itself. Every individual is created to engage himself in some activity at all levels and stages of his evolution. Howsoever one may try to run away from the world, there is no escape from activity. Physical withdrawal into solitude will not help since the mind cannot be at rest. Moreover, abandonment of action leads to a state of stupor and inertia which is a manifestation of the *Tamasic* element in us. In *Yoga Sutra* (C-I-30) the sage Patanjali describes the various obstacles, essentially psychosomatic, which a practising yogi has to guard against. The first five of them—disease, dullness, doubt, carelessness and laziness—are related to the Tamasic condition and they take us away from action and thus from life itself. Idleness, therefore, is the devil's workshop. On the other hand, if a man has many interests, wants or desires, he will be dissipating his energies in so many directions that they will lead him to indecision, failure and weakness. Everybody, who is born in the world, brings with him a certain nature (*prakriti* or *swabhava*). It represents the aggregate of his innate tendencies from which he is inseparable. Its hold is so strong that it constantly motivates a person to act in a certain way. This inherent nature determines one's aptitude in life and takes him towards self-fulfilment. Since it is not possible to escape one's prakriti, it is not possible to escape karma. The important thing to remember is that we should have the right attitude towards work and life. This is one of the prerequisites for a creative and peaceful way of living. Have an all absorbing goal in life towards which you can direct all your energies and develop the right attitude.

Our Action Potential

To understand our motives and impulses, ancient seers and yogis have classified motivation into four broad categories: *Dharma, Artha, Kama* and *Moksha*. We must remember that real yoga is applied yoga and it must be translated in terms of living actions and an attempt should be made to understand the real motivation behind our actions.

- Living by performing one's natural duties and responsibilities is called *Dharma* (responsibilities which are obligatory in relationships with others).
- Doing something to earn a living is *Artha* (we translate it here as barter or compensation).
- Doing something to enjoy oneself—*Kama* (all actions in the quest for pleasure through emotions or sex).
- Doing something to elevate oneself in life—*Moksha*. Actions performed in a spirit of altruism, associated with the noble quality of self-sacrifice such as unselfish love which has a deep subconscious feeling of service.

> *Unselfish love has enormous creative and therapeutic potential far greater than most people think.*
>
> — Sorokins

Acts of this kind elevate us and bring us nearer to the spiritual life and that leads to moksha—self-realisation.

These motivations are sometimes correlated with each other and sometimes occur in combination—a businessman may undertake a deal combining a pleasure trip; or a nurse working on a salary may have a touch of moksha; a temple priest may include all the four elements of motivation in the nature of his work. So, human actions may be prompted singly or in combination with these four motivations. The important thing is the awareness and clarity of motivation coupled with a clear understanding of *What you want* and *Why you want*. It is like fixing the centre of a circle.

How else can you draw a circle? Most of us remain confused or undecided about motivations or there may be a bifurcation of motivation by smaller objectives in life. Whenever the basic motivation is not strong or is disturbed, the result is less satisfactory, leaving the individual frustrated.

See that your major motivations do not get distorted and are not misused. Yoga promises fulfilment of any of your motivations but through the yoga means alone. While pleasure is legitimate, addiction to it occasions contempt and loss of wealth, besides causing physical and mental problems. Lust for money reduces a man to being an exploiter. Yoga holds that its aim is to direct the aspirant initially to control the artha and kama activities by the practice of dharma and moksha. The main theme and content of Indiana culture is integration and harmonisation of the diverse aspects of life (fourfold *purusharthas*) through which we proceed towards the ultimate realisation of our inner divine nature.

Begin to use this programme of thinking and acquire the habit of analysing your actions and activities of the body.

> ***Remember...***
> A strong motivation (M) is based on a value judgement (V). Only then is a proper attitude (A) cultivated which finally determines the behaviour (B) pattern.

31

The Importance of Karma Yoga

Do your duties remembering that you are only an instrument in the hands of God who is the final arbiter of all actions. With this attitude, the ego will be transcended, all karmas will become equal in your eyes and everything that you do will be divinised. Freedom in action is possible only if one is able to free oneself from the expectation of results. Karma in itself is not a source of bondage, it is the thoughts about the outcome, successful or otherwise, which cause all the trouble, since the mind constantly oscillates between the two opposite poles of success and defeat, delight and depression. There is no denying the fact that karma is a means to achieve a specific end. We have to understand that there is no point in bothering about the results since every karma will inevitably bring its destind result. No one can escape the law of karmic results. It is a different matter, however, that the resuits may not be in accordance with our expectations. In spite of our best efforts, the outcome may be partial or even adverse since there are so many factors at work, which are beyond our control. Things do not always happen the way we want them to happen. When we are engaged in our work we should keep in mind all the possibilities and try to exercise equanimity in the face of both success and failure. Preoccupation with results can be a big distraction in the right performance of the work at hand. Yoga has been described in the *Gita* as 'skill in action.' To perform well, what is needed is total absorption in the activity of the moment, with the physical, mental and vital forces acting in unison with a strong motivation to bring out the best in you. If a painter while painting is preoccupied with thoughts of money or fame, and a doctor while treating a serious case has his eye on the pocket, the performance will suffer since wholeheartedness towards the activity will be missing.

A true karmayogi combines deep interest with perfect detachment. Every moment of activity is a moment of accomplishment, of joy, since his joy lies in the activity itself, not in the fruits of activity. When we do our work out of love, there is no expectation since love is an act of giving—giving our best, our whole self spontaneously. In such a moment our self does not exist, only the pursuit of love exists and we become what we do. We are absolutely free and absolutely absorbed.

Remember...

- "It is not work that kills men," says Beecher, "it is worry."
- Our lives are humdrum, ordinary, mediocre, because we do not develop our inherent talents or potential.
- Duty must be performed regardless of its result, because it ought to be done. Engage yourself in your duty and work with a sense of total participation.
- The basic principle of human existence is that what we wish from others should be made the guideline of our own actions.
- Do not consider any work superior or inferior.
- Transcend the 'I'. Remember, you are not the doer but only an instrument of action.
- Cultivate faith in the Higher Reality of the Absolute and function as a part of the larger process of life.

Working for love is indeed freedom in action.

32
Attitude of Mind is Vital in Yoga

The attitude with which we look at life and at our problems makes all the difference. We can say either "the glass is half-full" or "the glass is half-empty." The former statement conveys a positive attitude and elates us while the latter conveys a pessimistic attitude and a sense of depression. It all depends on how you look at the situation—positively of negatively. It is the positive, hopeful, constructive mental attitude that accomplishes all the great things in the world and also acts as the best possible means of self-protection.

In yoga, the inner mental attitude we adopt towards anything governs our life and determines to a greater or lesser extent its effects upon us. For example, the last three *Niyamas* namely *Tapa* (fortitude), *Svadhyaya* (self-study), and *Ishvara Pranidhana* (Resignation to the will of the Absolute) correspond to the triple nature of a human being and develop in him certain attitudes related to his will, intellect and emotions respectively.

Tapa

Tapa stands for the mental attitude of fortitude. It refers to a mental quality wherein a man remains undisturbed by opposite conditions—joy and sorrow, pleasure and pain, love and hatred, gain or loss, success and failure. Man is caught in this play of the opposites and entangles himself in the process of wordly life and becomes miserable because he identifies himself with the mundane things without realising their ephemeral nature. Perils and misfortune and want, pain and injury are more or less the certain lot of every man who comes into this world. Remember, all sufferings are painfully effective tutors by which we gather all the strength to face crises in life. The only things we should guard against is not to take failure personally or consider it a personal dead end but take sufferings as blessings in disguise or adopt the attitude: "That every failure is a success put off for tomorrow; every success is a failure overcome." (Shri Yogendraji in *Life Problem.*)

It is this attitude of fortitude in man which will sustain him through the perils of life and develop in him a stronger will power. He will be able to maintain equanimity of mind in the face of both joyful and painful situations.

Svadhyaya (Self-study)

This is an essential stage in yogic development starting with an attitude of self-awareness and self-introspection in order to know oneself as thoroughly as possible.

If you are to begin with an attitude of witnessing your actions and reactions, many of the problems bothering you can be overcome easily. Not only that, this passive awareness, reflection and understanding of life will help you to develop an objective attitude in life with less egoistic attachment and passion.

Isvara-pranidhana (Resignation to the Will of the Absolute)

This implies devotion or surrender to God and resignation to His will. Submitting ourselves to the will of God is the only alternative left when tragedies or calamities engulf us. On such occasions argument and reason are of no avail. Surrender to Isvara acts as a psychological safety valve to cope with sad situations. Develop this feeling and attitude of surrender to him.

I.K. Taimni says, "When we surrender ourselves to Him completely and merge our consciousness we becomes desireless, because on becoming established in the very source of satisfaction of all desires, there is nothing left to be desired."

This is a sure way to lead a tension-free life. Remember adoption of an attitude of total surrender to God and turning our mind towards divine light can transform and spiritualise the material aspects of life.

The basic practical techniques of yoga outlined in the earlier chapter will help you acquire a healthy attitude towards self-development and emotional control.

Asanas
These are not merely mechanical postures. They are expressions of an attitude and experience to give you a positive feeling. They are all attitude-bound and contribute to steadiness and comfort.

Pranayamas
These demand an attitude of total attention and participation. While watching your breathing, do it softly and smoothly without any jerks. At the same time, equalise your breathing-in and breathing-out.

Psychosomatic Practices for Relaxation
These develop an attitude of 'Letting go' your body completely to the floor. They help the body to rejuvenate its store of energy and give rest to its overworked parts.

Remember, relaxation is not an activity; it is an attitude, a way of harmony and balance. You can take things easy and you are not too much subjectively involved.

Meditation
Meditation, which contributes steadiness and calmness of the mind, develops a state of peace and an objective attitude to life. This will help us to drive away disappointments, restlessness, anxiety and fear. We remain silent witnesses to the external changes in our environment. We perform our duties more efficiently.

33
On Faith

Cultivation of faith is important. When we submit ourselves completely to the care of a physician whom we trust, we are showing faith. The placebo—an imitation medicine or a dummy drug—has brought about a revolution in the theory and practice of medicine. Patients treated with placebos have often shown better results than those administered genuine drugs. It has been proved that placebos have curative powers and can be as effective as drugs and at times, more effective than drugs. It clearly shows, says Norman Cousins, "how the human body heals itself and the mysterious ability of the brain leads biochemical changes that are essential for combating diseases." A patient's faith in medicine or in the doctor is far more important than the pill prescribed for him. Faith is the great antidote for worry. We are afraid because we cannot see our way out. "Tagore tells us that when a mother is feeding her child on the breast, she may shift the child from one breast to another. The child starts crying. To the child at that moment it is a loss. But the mother knows better. She is actually providing more nourishment."

Faith seeks the way. Faith keeps a man from worrying and enables him to use his resourcefulness to an infinitely greater advantage. There can be no fear of poverty or failure when the mind is dominated by faith. Where faith is, there is courage, there is fortitude, there is steadfastness and strength.

34
Belief in a Higher Benevolent Reality

Faith is like a mother who nourishes the seeker of self-improvement and tends him throughout his spiritual development. Many psychiatrists acknowledge the role of faith in helping an individual to accept himself and his environment. Yoga cultivates a positive attitude of acceptance—acceptance that there is a larger reality and that we are but a small part of a larger process. Faith in something bigger than oneself is indeed the cornerstone of the belief in a Superior Reality that pervades everything. It is this belief in the Absolute that gives a meaning to our life which is otherwise lived in fragments. It also provides a built-in immunity and the individual is at peace with himself and his surroundings.

"In fact such a belief in a Higher Benevolent Reality may then grow into a full-fledged philosophy of life. We may be able to explain to ourselves many of this apparently insoluble problem we face. We may gain clarity and derive more meaning out of life." Dr Jayadeva Yogendra says, "This world process is like a big wheel of a machine—each aspect of life being related to another. We are beneficiaries of this process and in turn contributors to its smooth rotation. We do not run the show; we are merely a part of a process—a process that is intrinsically good." Hold on to this attitude.

A man who believes that there is a power infinitely wiser than him which is directing and guiding the affairs of the universe does not lose his balance of mind when disappointments, losses, reverses, catastrophies come his way. His faith looks beyond misfortune and sees the sun behind the clouds, the victory beyond the seeming defeat. To him, in the words of Shree Shree Ma Anandamayie, "nothing happens which is not an expression of God's Grace".

35
Steps for Self-Improvement

Acceptance
More than half of your problems can be solved if you accept a person the way he or she is. Remember, it is not easy to mould someone to your way of thinking.

The moment we enter the precincts of this world we find that we are not only individual entities but are placed in relation to certain people and circumstances beyond our control. Initially, it is the family towards which we have certain obligatory duties which have to be accepted without resentment. You have to learn to accept things as they come, without getting agitated about them and patiently wait for the change to come. The escapist tendency will not take you anywhere; you have to learn to accept reality. Accept what you cannot change. In a happy marriage, husband and wife accept each other as they are and it is a better way of adjustment; similarly, in friendship. Most important, accept yourself as you are.

Adjustment and Adaptation
Life demands adjustment if we are to live in harmony with ourselves and with our environment, whether at home or at the place of work. Personal adjustment involves a certain flexibility of outlook and a skill for better adaptability so that you feel at ease in any situation and can avoid extreme reactions. At home, there is adjustment between husband and wife and other members of the family making allowances for human weaknesses and frailties. Do

not run after what you do not possess but adjust and adapt yourself to what you already possess.

Stop Blaming Others
The first sign of maturity is elimination of criticism. Do not go through life looking for trouble, for faults and failures, for the crooked, the ugly, and the deformed, do not see the distorted man—see the man that God made. Just make up your mind firmly at the very outset in life that you will not criticise or condemn others, or find fault with their mistakes and shortcomings. Instead look for likeable and admirable qualities in people. Remember, do not judge anyone nor condemn anyone.

Develop your own Inherent Potential
Discover your own inherent potential and develop it to the maximum. This will give you a sense of satisfaction. Do not get carried away by external influences or opinions of others and do not follow the dictum "Monkey sees—monkey does". Chose your own path and walk on it with a strong motivation. Also work steadfastly with devotion and a spirit of excellence—you are not only bound to succeed but you will achieve the full flowering of your true personality. This will give a positive direction to your creative urges and it will fill your life with joy and happiness. According to Sri Aurobindo, true education "helps the growing soul to draw out that which is best and make it perfect for a noble use."

Live in the Now
The future is unknown and unknowable. To live in the future is just as unrealistic as to live in the past which is gone and dead. Keep your mind on what you have and manage the present, living in the *Now*. Take real and lively interest in life—your job, your home, your family, your hobbies, social affairs and friends. Never live your life hurriedly; rather enjoy the life process and find beauty in simple things. Live vitally, sincerely, fully and dynamically in the *Present*.

On Relationships
In order to follow the yoga way, we have to cultivate:
- Friendliness towards those who are happy.
- Compassion for those who are unhappy.
- Joyful participation with those who are virtuous.
- Indifference towards those who are evil-minded.

This fourfold statement of Patanjali for better adjustment in life covers practically the whole gamut of human relationships. If we follow this advice, we will be able to live in harmony with others and keep our mind calm and steady.

Happiness
- "Be good and you will be happy" is a very old piece of sound advice.
- Happiness comes by giving happiness to others.
- A job well done gives satisfaction and happiness.
- A real feeling of fulfilment and contentment gives happiness.
- Self-help and self-reliance will give you happiness. Above all, remember the source of happiness is within us and so do not expect happiness to come from outside, from external things and material possessions.

Harmony
Create harmony in such a manner that you are at peace not only with your own self but also with your environment. Harmony is the first step towards health, happiness and peace.

Strike balance and harmony in all the activities of life. Cultivation of inner peace creates inner harmony.

Remember the words of an eminent doctor, Dr Edward Bach, who has said, "We must steadfastly practise peace, imagining our minds as a lake ever to be kept calm, without waves or even ripples to disturb its tranquillity, and gradually develop this state of peace until no event of life, no circumstance, no other personality is able, under any condition, to ruffle the surface of that lake or raise within it any feelings of irritability, depression or doubt."

Reaction Pattern

"We have the choice," says Dr John A Schindler, M D between reacting with equanimity, resignation, courage, determination and cheerfulness on the one hand and with grabbiness, grumbling, worry and apprehension on the other. The choice is yours right now."

Cheerfulness

"Cheerfulness is the most important factor in the maintenance of health and the cure of disease", says Dr A J Sanderson. "Its power to do good like a medicine is not an artificial stimulation of the tissue, which is followed by reaction and greater waste, as in the case with many drugs; but the effect of cheerfulness is an actual life-giving influence through a normal channel, the results of which reach every part of the system."

A good hearty laugh expands the chest and makes the blood bound merrily along.

Epilogue
An Ideal Synthesis
The Obvious Solution—Body-Mind-Spirit Culture

Dr Shanti Auluck[*]

Beauty lies in harmony—harmony of forms, colours, sounds, etc. There is a harmony of mind too—a mind that experiences joy and happiness free from conflicts, anxieties and a sense of inadequacy. Occasionally, we all experience it but for a brief time. Harmony is not only beautiful and pleasing but it is the crux of life too. In the words of biologists, "A living organism is not an aggregate; life is organisation. Any integrated and organised system can function effectively only when its various components work in harmony and coordination. Man is an organised whole composed of body and mind. Both are intimately linked and capable of deeply influencing each other. A harmonious functioning of both is essential for a life that releases the creative potential in us, gives us a sense of fulfilment and joyful existence.

Mind Affects the Body

That the body affects the mind is known to us. But the fact that the mind can also affect the body is not equally well known. The discoveries made about the functioning of the nervous system and its relationship with the rest of the body have amply demonstrated this truth. Researches in the field of neuropsychology and

---

[*] Lecturer in Psychology, LSR College, New Delhi.

Epilogue

psychophysiology have revealed some salient features of the interaction between mind and body. These are:

- Whenever one is anxious, worried or agitated, one's heart starts pumping harder, blood pressure rises.
- Chronic anxiety, worry, or an agitated state of mind disturbs the homeostasis and lowers the efficiency of one's body as well as mind.
- Mental states influence the immune system also. Negative emotions like worry and tension lower the efficiency of the immune system to fight infections.
- Some areas in the brain secrete a chemical called endorphin that brightens one's mood, mitigates pain and promotes the body's own internal healing processes. Neuroscientists suggest that changes in breathing can alter the flow and concentration of endorphins—a fact that yogis in our country knew long ago.
- Study of the brain reveals that in a calm and peaceful state of mind, the higher centres of the brain can carry out their functions more effectively resulting in coherent thinking, clearer perception and improved memory functions.

The body carries out several functions, eg., digestion, respiration, blood circulation, synthesis of required proteins and other substances and elimination of the waste and toxic substances. These are interdependent systems and their integration is provided by the nervous system and the endocrine system. These are considered to be the communication network of the body and are controlled by the brain. Figure 18 shows their interrelationship with all the major organs of the body. It also indicates a two-way interaction between the centres for cognitive functions and emotions, too, ie., thinking can alter emotions. Here is a clue to modifying the emotional states of the mind through the control of thought processes. However, emotions too can alter and subdue the functioning of the higher centres, ie., thinking and perception. We see that happening in moments of heightened emotions when we find ourselves unable to concentrate and think clearly.

Inner Strength: Harmonious Functioning of the Mind

It is well known that bodily organs can work effectively only in a harmonious internal environment known as homeostasis. Physical health is possible when homeostatic functions are intact, which results in strength, increased stamina to work and resistance to fight disease causing agents in the body. Similar is the case with the mind. The mind functions better when there is harmony in it.

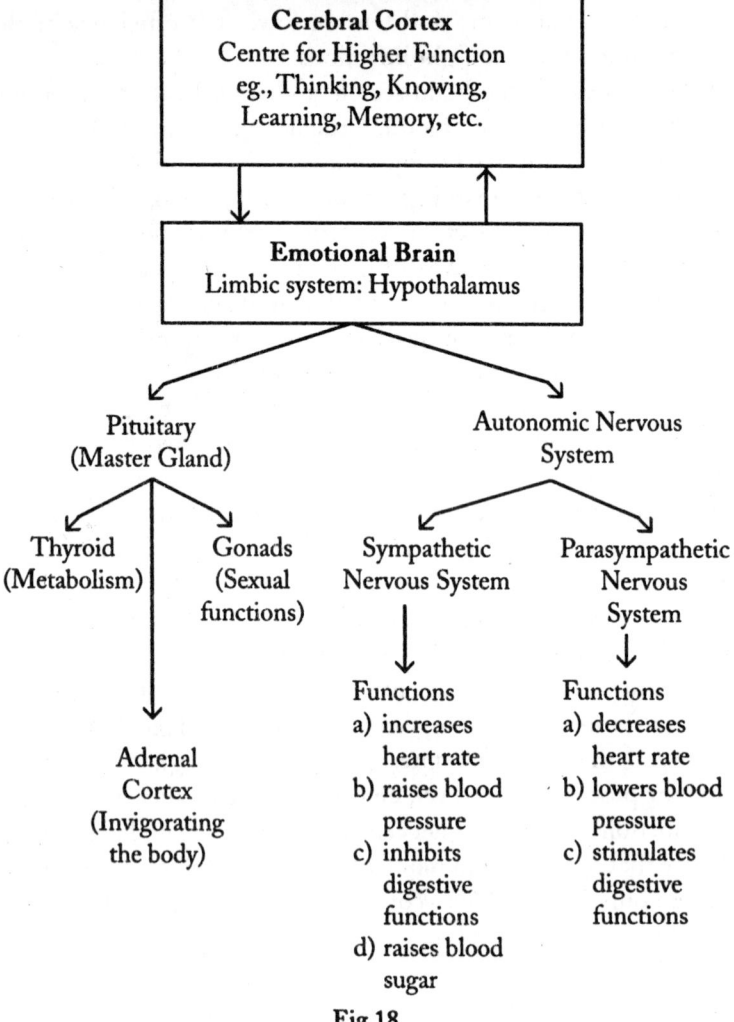

Fig 18

TABLE 1

Negative Tendencies	Positive Tendencies
1. Fear	1. Compassion
2. Confusion	2. Fearlessness
3. Sense of worthlessness and inadequacy	3. Clarity of thought
4. Agitated mind tossed by various emotions	4. Inner peace, equanimity
5. Fragmentation of thought, feeling and action	5. Emotional maturity
6. Lack of control over oneself	6. Self-discipline
7. Egocentricity	7. Acceptance of reality
8. Escapist	8. Accommodative

Inner harmony is reflected in a serene and quiet mind, which is at peace with itself. It generates inner strength which gives one the courage to face the problems of life. Table 1 summarises the negative and positive tendencies in us. Overcoming the negative and gradually moving towards the positive ones help in cultivating inner strength.

How do we bring about this change in us? None of us are born with it. Each one of us has to work it out. This requires introspection and self-reflection. Honest self-examination is a prerequisite for self-improvement. To make a beginning in this direction would necessitate a clear understanding of the nature of problems and how and why they arise.

The Nature of Problems

What are the problems we commonly experience in our daily living? We are unhappy with people around us; we are unhappy with the circumstances in which we find ourselves—our job, home, financial status, desire for recognition, ill-treatment by others, jealousy, competition, sense of worthlessness, etc. There is always a sense of inadequacy present in us in one way or the other. By worrying over what we do not have, we fail to enjoy what we have. A closer look at our miseries and unhappiness would reveal that to some extent we ourselves are responsible for it. The source of the problems, as well as their solution, lies within ourselves.

Contradictions within and wide gaps between thought and action are bound to disrupt inner peace. Unrealistic perceptions and expectations cause agitations within. Seeking approval without rather than within would not allow us to gain stability. Inaccurate perceptions about ourselves and others prevent us from getting in touch with our inner self and forming healthy relationships with others. All these are very important sources which create a disturbed state of mind and cloud our thinking.

If we analyse ourselves closely, we will find that the whole world revolves around our own self, the 'I' or the 'Ego'. Our whole effort is to protect it; happiness/unhappiness depends upon how events seem to be enhancing or depreciating it. In *Brihadaranya Upanishad* is said - "Not indeed for the love of all is all dear, but for the love of the self is all dear." A noted Buddhist Monk, G K Gyatso has said, "All the fearful aspects of *samsara* from the greatest down to the smallest arise from the self-cherishing attitudes." Here lies the crux of the problem. The protection of self-image is of paramount importance to all of us. We are all the time trying to establish our own selves in the eyes of others as well as to ourselves. In this process our appreciation of reality is dimmed. We tend to protect our ego at all costs. The mechanisms which we generally employ to protect the ego are termed by psychology as defence mechanisms. Table II provides a brief description of these defences which people generally employ to protect themselves from hurts and insults. They are not necessarily conscious; rather they operate subconsciously or unconsciously.

These defence mechanisms are ordinarily used in combination rather than singly. They are normal adjustive reactions unless used in an exaggerated form. They soften failure, alleviate anxiety and hurt and protect one's feelings of worth and adequacy. They operate on relatively automatic and habitual levels but they do involve some measure of self-deception and reality distortion. They distort our perception of the reality and change it in such a way that it becomes more agreeable to us.

Another problem is that often our judgements about ourselves are not based on self-analysis and understanding but on the basis of how others evaluate us. We judge ourselves by our successes and failures, by the appreciation or criticism of others, because we are not firmly rooted in the knowledge arising from our own self-examination and understanding whereby we can know our strengths as well as limitations.

This lack of introspection and self-awareness results in non-recognition of the exact nature of problems. The lack of courage to face a situation creates avoidance behaviour which only temporarily eases the problem but in the long run weakens our inner strength.

Seeking Solutions Within

An effective way to solve the problem is to seek the causes which give rise to them. These may lie within us or in external situations. Temporary solutions will only suppress them. The problem will keep reappearing from time to time.

There is, need to look within ourselves, to see our own motives, emotions, thoughts and actions in order to know if they are giving rise to certain problems. Problems also arise externally without our contributing to them. Most of the time they arise from both these factors: our faulty perceptions and attitude as well as external circumstances. Where the changes are possible and needed, one has to gather the courage to make them. If things are beyond our control, then we have to develop acceptance. But careful thinking is required, otherwise we may be unnecessarily fighting with situations or else giving up too soon to compromise with them.

In order to generate resources within to face difficult situations effectively we need to:
- Recognise the problem.
- Become aware of one's motives and expectations.
- Make an effort to be objective because emotions often colour our perceptions and thinking.
- See the relevance and appropriateness of our conduct.
- Try to see the situation from others' point of view.
- Show concern and respect for others' views and feelings.
- Make an effort to develop perseverance and forbearance.

TABLE II

Denial of Reality
The simplest and most primitive of all self-defence mechanisms is denial of reality, in which an attempt is made to screen out disagreeable realities by ignoring or refusing to acknowledge them, eg., turning away from unpleasant issues, refusing to discuss them.

Fantasy
This is a mechanism by which frustration is overcome by the imaginary achievement of goals and meeting of needs.

Repression
This refers to the exclusion of threatening or painful thoughts and experiences from consciousness. It works without our being aware of it.

Rationalisation
This refers to justifying our wrong-doing by giving reasons for it. It does not arise from serious thinking and reasoning. The purpose is to prove oneself, one's views and actions for example, the story of "Sour Grapes".

Projection
Here others are seen as responsible for one's own shortcomings, mistakes and misdeeds and also for one's unacceptable impulses, thoughts and desires. In fights one often sees people blaming each other for their acts of aggression.

Displacement
This refers to shifting one's emotions, eg., anger and anxieties, etc., from the person or the object towards which it was originally directed to another person or object. For example, a fight with someone shows up in our annoyance with other people in a different situation.

Epilogue

Regression
This refers to behavioural characteristics of some earlier stages of development. This is commonly referred to as childish or immature behaviour.

Undoing
This refers to negation of disapproved thoughts or actions by some kind of penance. It is like subjecting oneself to punishment for the wrongs one has committed with a view to relieving oneself of this guilt.

Identification
This refers to deriving importance by attaching/identifying oneself with important and powerful people or groups, thereby seeking glory and ridding oneself of one's sense of inadequacy and deficiency.

Compensation
Compensatory reactions are defences against feelings of inferiority and inadequacy growing out of real or imaginary personal defects as well as out of our failures. Such reactions may be constructive or debilitating: constructive when our shortcomings motivate us to excel in some field of human endeavour, and unhealthy when we try to show off in order to hide our sense of insecurity. This kind of behaviour may also show in an over-critical attitude when we tend to state that others are not really good, thereby trying to prove our worth by showing their faults.

Dr Jayadeva Yogendraji has said,

> *Yoga is basically an art of living. In yoga we learn to accept life as it is. We seek a meaning in it. We create a trust in nature. The larger process of life is good. We should find our place in this process. Let us not sit idle and think negatively. Let us not remain at war with life. We should rather remain involved in the business of living.*

The vision of yoga and the entire philosophical thought in India has something more to reveal about man. According to it, man is not body and mind alone. There is a deeper reality which forms the essential/spiritual nature of man. What we consider self/ego is a case of misplaced identity and is in fact the accumulated conditionings of the past. One of the aphorisms in Patanjali's *Yogasutra* (Sutra 287 Sadhana Panda) says:

Yogāṅgānuṣṭhānād aśuddhi-kṣaye
jñānadiptir ā viveka-khyātek.

The purpose of the discipline of yoga is to eliminate the impurities caused by the process of conditioning so that the light of pure unconditioned awareness may shine.

That is the height of human perfection. Yoga provides an integrated approach to attaining it and emphasises the body and mind culture which paves the way for a fuller life—a life of harmony, joy and creativity.

Bibliography

Bach, Edward. *Heal Thyself.* Rochford: The C. W. Daniel Co. Ltd., 1957

Banerjee, A. Kumar. *Nath Yoga.* Digvijayanath Trust, Gorakhnath Temple, Gorakhpur.

Benjamin, Harry. *Commence Vegetarianism.* Northants: Thorsons Publishers Ltd., 1972.

Coleman, James. *Abnormal Psychology and Modern Life.* Scott Foresman & Co., 1956.

Cousins, Norman. *Anatomy of an Illness.* New York: Bantam Books, 1979.

Dangayach, K. B. *About Vegetarian Diet.* Vol. xxi, No 1, Bombay: *Journal of the Yoga Institute*, 1975.

Guide to a Fuller Life. Bombay: Yogendra Publications, The Yoga Institute, 1986.

Mangalvedkar. *The Philosophy of Action.* Madras: B. G. Tilka's Githa Rahasya, The Indian Literature Pub., 1923

Marden, Orison Swett. *The Miracle of Right Thought.* V. Kalyanaram Iyer & Co., 1925.

Marden, Orison Swett. *Making Friends with Our Nerves.* London: Rider & Co., 1926.

Marden, Orison Swett. *Cheerfulness.* London: Paternoster House, E.C.

Marden, Orison Swett. *Every Man a King.* V. Kalyanaram Iyer & Co., 1923.

Nath, Pt. Shambhu. *Speaking of Yoga — A Practical Guide to Better Living.* New Delhi: Sterling Publishers Pvt. Ltd., 1988.

6. Yogendra Pranayama No 2 (standing)	Start with easy counts, reach gradually to 8	10 rounds
7. Vakrasana to start Exh.	Inh. Exh. Inh. 3 : 6 : 3	4 times
8. Yoga Mudra in Sukhasana to start INH	Exh. Susp. Inh. 3 : 6 : 3	3 rounds
9. Bhujangasana	Inh. Ret. Exh. 3 : 6 : 3	5 times
10. Yoni Mudra	Normal breathing	10 minutes Start with 5, gradually increase to 10 minutes
11. Savasana or Makarasana	Normal breathing	7/10 minutes

(c) Afternoon: after Lunch

Yogendra Nishpanda Bhava (Meditation)	Normal breathing	10/15 minutes

Note: Listen to the sound either of the fan, cooler or airconditioner in summer, blower in winter; rhythmic sound of low intensity; wall clock, traffic sound or a recorded cassette of a rhythmic sound, etc.

(d) Evening

Housewifes after tea; for working men and women after they return home.

1. Yogendra Pranayama No 4 (lying down position)	Start with easy count of 5/6 reach to a maximum of 8 seconds	2 minutes
2. Savasana	Normal breathing	10 minutes

Appendix

(E) At Night: Before going to Bed

1. Yoni Mudra or   10 minutes
   Y. Nishpanda
   Bhava or
   Sukhasana

   +

2. Ajapa Japa   3 minutes

   +

3. Contemplation —   5 minutes
   Fill your mind
   with (*Bhavana*)
   positive thoughts

Appendix

Health Care Course for Stress Management
(Men and Women)

(A) Early Morning
Chanting of *Aum* - 5 Minutes } to establish a link with
Gayatri Japa - 5 Minutes } the Supreme Spirit

(B) Before Breakfast

Guide Table — *40 Minutes a Day*

Sequence of Yoga Postures	Yogendra Rhythm	Frequency (Rounds/Times)
1. Sukhasana or Vajrasana (alter each day)	Normal breathing Inh. Ret. Exh.	5 minutes
2. Talasana I, II Var	3 : 6 : 3	6 times each
3. Konasana	3 : 6 : 3	4 times alternate bending each side
4. Trikonasana	Exh. Susp. Inh. 3 : 6 : 3	4 times
5. Yogendra Pranayama No 1 (standing)	Start with easy counts, reach gradually to 10	10 rounds

Parameshwaran, C. *The Grandeur of Gayatri.* New World Order Publications, 1949.

Pranayama Made Easy. The Yoga Sadhakas, Bombay: Yogendrra Publications, The Yoga Institute, 1981.

Sequeira, H. *Reducing Tensions.* Vol xxv, No. 9. Bombay: *Journal of the Yoga Institute,* 1980.

Sequeira, H. *Stability of Mind,* Vol. xxiv, No. 7. Bombay: *Journal of the Yoga Institute,* 1984.

Singh, S. J. *Food Remedies.* Lucknow: The All India Nature Cure Association, 1947.

Shri Yogendra. *Yoga Essays.* Bombay: The Yoga Institute, 1973.

Shri Yogendra. *Hatha Yoga Simplified.* Bombay: The Yoga Institute, 1975.

Shri Yogendra. *Guide to Yoga Meditation:* Bombay: Yogendra Publication Fund, 1983.

Tranquil State of Mind of the Gita. Vol xx, No 11, Bombay: *Journal of the Yoga Institute,* 1975.

Wenger, M. A., Jones F. N., Jones, M. H., *Physiological Psychology.* New York: University of California, 1956.

Wood, Ernest. *Yoga.* London: Pelican Original - Penguin Books rpt. 1968.

Yoga Today - Vol iii, No 1, Shri Yogendra Yoga Foundation, January-March 1981.

Yogi, Ramacharaka. *Hatha Yoga.* Bombay: D. B. Taraporevala Sons & Co., Asian Ppt. 1977.

Jayadeva, Yogendra. *How to Carry on Your Work.* Vol xxi, No. 10, Bombay: *Journal of the Yoga Institute,* May 1975.

Journal of the Yoga Institute. Vol xi, No 10, May 1966.

Vol xii, No 5, Dec 1967.

Vol xiv, No 11, June 1969.

Vol xx, No 8, March 1975.

Vol xxii, No 3, October, 1976.

Vol xix, No 11, June 1974.

Other Titles on Yoga

- Yoga — An Easy Approach
  by Prem Bhatia
- Speaking of Yoga — A Practical Guide
  by Pt. Shambhu Nath
- Speaking of Yoga and Nature Cure Therapy
  by K. S. Joshi
- Stress — An Owner's Manual
  by Arthur Rowshan

All You Wanted To Know About...

- Yoga
- Yoga for Health and Happiness
- Stress & Anger
- Anxiety
- Meditation
- Hatha Yoga
- Kriya Yoga
- Kundalini
- Chakras and Nadis